Confronting
a Church
in Controversy

Confronting
a Church
in Controversy

Bradford E. Hinze

Paulist Press
New York / Mahwah, NJ

A revised version of chapter 6 appeared as "Can We Find A Way Together? The Challenge of Synodality in a Wounded and Wounding Church" in *Irish Theological Quarterly* 85, no. 3 (2020): 215–29. DOI: 10.1177/0021140020926595 journals.sagepub.com/home/itq.

Cover design by Sharyn Banks
Book design by Lynn Else

Library of Congress Cataloging-in-Publication Data
Names: Hinze, Bradford E., 1954– author.
Title: Confronting a church in controversy / Bradford E. Hinze.
Description: New York / Mahwah, NJ : Paulist Press, [2022] | Includes bibliographical references and index. | Summary: "The aim of this book is to provide a reliable framework and theological orientation for considering the central factors that have contributed to the clergy sex abuse controversy in order to face the detrimental repercussions for the future of the church and to explore realistic responses based on an assessment of the various issues involved"—Provided by publisher.
Identifiers: LCCN 2021031978 (print) | LCCN 2021031979 (ebook) | ISBN 9780809155088 (paperback) | ISBN 9781587689079 (ebook)
Subjects: LCSH: Catholic Church—Clergy—Sexual behavior. | Child sexual abuse—Religious aspects—Catholic Church. | Child sexual abuse by clergy. | Sexual misconduct by clergy. | Sex crimes—Religious aspects—Catholic Church.
Classification: LCC BX1912.9 .H56 2022 (print) | LCC BX1912.9 (ebook) | DDC 261.8/3272—dc23
LC record available at https://lccn.loc.gov/2021031978
LC ebook record available at https://lccn.loc.gov/2021031979

ISBN 978-0-8091-5508-8 (paperback)
ISBN 978-1-58768-907-9 (e-book)

Published by Paulist Press
997 Macarthur Boulevard
Mahwah, New Jersey 07430
www.paulistpress.com

Printed and bound in the
United States of America

For Paul and Karl
with love, admiration, and pride

Contents

Contents

Preface

The title of this book, *Confronting a Church in Controversy*, is based on the name of a popular course at Fordham University initially designed by my colleague Brenna Moore, a great teacher with expertise in modern Catholicism, theology, and social movements. This class has also been taught by a number of my colleagues and doctoral students, as well as by me. Over a semester, when I have taught this course, we explore a range of controversies that have arisen during the last century in the Catholic Church, especially conflicts after the Second Vatican Council, which took place between 1962 and 1965. The chosen topics frequently involve controversies relating to gender and sexuality, such as the church's rejection of the use of artificial birth control in marriage, the prohibition of abortion, the mandatory requirement of celibacy in the ordination of men to the priesthood, and a spectrum of issues pertaining to homosexuality, including gay marriage. These classes also reflect upon the church's history with regard to racism toward African Americans but also toward people in North America who come from Latin American and Caribbean nations as well as Indigenous Native Americans.

This course provides students an opportunity to wrestle with conflicts they have experienced in the Catholic Church, in other Christian churches, or in other religious traditions. Typically, some students in the class are actively and comfortably involved in their faith traditions; but some are struggling with their faith, while others are no longer active or affiliated. It is also common to find that a few students have never been initiated into any religious tradition. Regardless of how the students self-identify in relation to religion, however, most quickly become intrigued with and engaged in discussing these controversies.

I've been amazed at how personally engaged and invested students are in their conversations with one another—in pairs, small groups, or with the entire class—about the topics and the assigned readings. It is impressive how honest they can be about their reactions and their opinions about what is at stake in these controversies: for themselves and their peers, for their families and communities, for the Catholic Church, for other religious communities, and for society at large. After a couple of weeks in the class the students are often increasingly willing to show their cards; and there are moments when it seems everyone is invested, and something important is happening as participants reveal what particular controversies mean to them and, often, how these issues affect them personally. I hope this book, like this course, creates a space and a time to think and talk about difficult topics that some individuals, families, schools, and religious communities consider taboo or find difficult to discuss.

While by definition all the controversies we cover in this class are hard topics, the one set of issues covered in this book is perhaps the most excruciating and challenging both to understand and to talk about. Our aversion to talking about this issue is one reason why it is necessary in the first place. The sexual abuse of children, women, and men by priests, and actions taken by their supervising bishops and cardinals to avoid scandal through concealment, deception, and suppression of these heinous actions by their clergy, are made possible by widespread adherence to a pernicious code of secrecy and silence.

Our contemporary discussion of clergy sex abuse and episcopal concealment deals largely with events that took place beginning in the second half of the twentieth century, escalated between 1965 and 1985, and have received increasing public attention and scrutiny since then, first especially in the United States and more recently worldwide. This particular book contributes to a wider attempt in this period to break through the code of silence by giving special attention to one aspect of this controversy: sexual abuse of minors by Catholic priests.

Preface

Three priests in the United States, all repeat sexual offenders against children, have become recognized as the most egregious perpetrators of clergy sex abuse against children in the later twentieth century. All three were brought to the attention of Catholics and non-Catholics alike in the United States and around the world by horrific stories of abuse that were reported on and repeated in newspapers, on television news shows, and in many secular and religious media outlets between 1985 and 2002. These stories of individual priests initiated a subsequent wave of discoveries about bishops' and cardinals' complicity in making these recurring violations possible. To introduce this historical context and time frame, I will give here the most basic details of the criminal profiles of these priests.

Gilbert Gauthe was the first contemporary priest to gain widespread public notoriety as a sex abuser. Ordained in Lafayette, Louisiana, in 1972, he started molesting children that same year, eventually repeating these crimes in four different parish settings. Finally, after a decade of abusive behavior, criminal allegations were made, and on August 12, 1983, he was removed from priestly ministry. In 1985 he was convicted of abusing thirty-nine children, but many believe that he had victimized far more. Gauthe was the first priest to face a criminal trial and conviction for sexually abusing minors. Released from prison after ten years, he subsequently abused a three-year-old child and was arrested again.[1]

James Porter was ordained in 1960 for the diocese of Fall River, Massachusetts. In 1993 he was convicted of molesting twenty-eight minors, but he admitted to abusing over one hundred victims in various states, including Minnesota, Texas, and New Mexico. He was removed from the priesthood ("laicized") in 1974, but his church superiors did not report him to the police, and his criminal behavior did not stop. It wasn't until the 1990s that one of his victims contacted law officials and began networking with other victims in an attempt to bring Porter to justice. Only after the victims' allegations were reported on in the *Boston Globe* in May 1992 and in a national television news show were criminal charges brought against Porter. He was eventually sentenced to eighteen to twenty years in prison.

John Geoghan, who was ordained in 1962, became perhaps the world's most notorious clergy abuser due to the series of articles published by the *Boston Globe* beginning January 6, 2002. He was accused of sexually abusing eighty-seven children in more than 150 incidents. The investigation of Geoghan's criminal behavior by the *Globe's* "Spotlight" team led to the discovery of not only a wider pattern of clergy sex abuse of minors in the Archdiocese of Boston, but also a range of actions and inactions by Cardinal Bernard Law and his assistant bishops that comprised a spectrum of acts of mismanagement and malfeasance. Most notably, the *Globe's* reporters discovered, abusive priests were commonly moved to different parishes in the archdiocese or other dioceses, or temporarily to medical and psychological treatment centers, rather than being held accountable either by following the procedures of canon law or through civil criminal and legal procedures. Subsequent investigations across the world have found similar patterns, and it has also become clear that many times, known "problem" priests were shuffled to parishes or territories with predominantly immigrant, poor, often people of color, all with less power to complain. In other cases, abusive priests accumulated power within their home dioceses, making it less likely that their behavior would be checked by their fellow clergy.

While writing this book I reached one conclusion about its subject matter. This inference, obvious for anyone who spends time on this issue, surfaced when I was writing chapter 2, "Anatomy of a Pathology." The problems, difficulties, and systemic issues operative in the church that have come to light in these cases of clergy sex abuse of minors provide a template and a prism that can also illuminate different, sometimes intersecting, controversies that also wound people who are or have been active in the church, and they reveal associated social pathologies and dysfunctions in church institutions. This hypothesis can also be formulated historically or archeologically: certain harmful dynamics in the church over the past fifty years have contributed to and may be culminating in the kinds of problems associated with clergy sex abuse. How Catholics confront the controversy of clergy sex abuse of minors, therefore, can provide insight into how they might confront other conflicts and controversies in the church.

The first chapter offers three overlapping composite sketches of victims who have been sexually abused by priests and of how this behavior has been concealed by bishops, cardinals, and other superiors in religious orders such as the Jesuits or the Dominicans. The second chapter explores contrasting and complementary interdisciplinary approaches to the personal and collective forms of corruption and disease that have led to these criminal behaviors. Chapter 3 introduces four of the most influential groups voicing prophetic critiques of clergy sex abuse: the victim-survivors themselves; a group of allies known as Voice of the Faithful; media witnesses, here represented by the *Boston Globe* "Spotlight" investigative reporters; and grand jury advocates. Each of these groups is an example of a style of prophetic witness, protest, and, in a couple of cases, the development of social movements aimed at systemic change.

The book then explores the responses developed by the institutional church. Chapter 4 reconstructs a selection of the most important teachings, canonical policies, and practices developed by both the United States Conference of Catholic Bishops and the three popes who have attempted reforms to address this controversy: John Paul II, Benedict XVI, and Francis. Chapter 5 provides the readers an opportunity to reflect on kinds of responses to clergy abuse that are often resisted but that should be openly discussed. The book concludes with chapter 6, which asks if and how we can find our collective way in a "wounded and wounding church." My hope in writing this book is that readers, whether individuals or classes of students such as those at Fordham, Catholics or non-Catholics, and people who are religiously disaffiliated from any religious community yet who are spiritual seekers, will be able to use this book as a jumping-off point for careful, serious, deep conversations about both its immediate topic, clergy sex abuse of minors, and the broader question of how we can talk about and address deeply painful topics within our communities.

Acknowledgments

I did not expect to write this book. I was asked by an editor at Paulist Press to take on such a project in October 2018, at a time when a new wave of attention to the crisis of clergy sexual abuse of minors in the church and episcopal malfeasance was emerging. This increased awareness was precipitated by two events: the public announcement in June 2018 that the Archdiocese of New York Review Board had a confirmed case of sexual abuse of a person who was a minor when the crime occurred involving Cardinal Theodore McCarrick; and two months later, on August 14th, the release of the Pennsylvania Grand Jury Report on Clergy Abuse.

A month before receiving this invitation from Paulist Press, in September 2018, I had received another request, this one from Paul Lakeland, then president of the Catholic Theological Society of America (CTSA), to convene a group of theologians to identify the central theological issues that merit attention in response to the scandal of clergy sex abuse of minors. Lakeland and the Board of Directors of the CTSA appointed the following theologians for this commission: Christina Astorga, James Coriden, Natalia Imperatori-Lee, Teresia Hinga, Kristin Heyer, and Julie Rubio. We engaged in periodic conversations over six months; and these wise colleagues' views have influenced my own analysis in this investigation.

The entire book went through a major revision after January 2019, when I took on the position of principal investigator of a major project entitled Taking Responsibility: Jesuit Educational Institutions Confront the Causes and Legacy of Clergy Sexual Abuse, an initiative of Fordham University. This project, designed and initiated by J. Patrick Hornbeck and Christine Firer Hinze and supported by major funding from a private family foundation, has provided opportunities to learn from leading-edge research currently being conducted by teams of scholars at Jesuit universities across the United States. Georgetown University, for example, inspired by the university's recovery of the history and repercussions of their Jesuit community's historical involvement in slavery, is championing the need to follow the lead of victim survivors and to develop ways to amplify the pedagogical and institutional impact of their narratives. Gonzaga University is conducting research focused on marginalized communities of color, especially Native American Indians, who have suffered from clergy abuse. Xavier University is investigating the psychological and theological-ethical implications of the moral injury suffered by victim-survivors of clergy abuse and the various individuals and groups of people that have been harmed as a result. Santa Clara University/Jesuit School of Theology is conducting a theological and social-psychological study of clergy formation programs, attuned to addressing the causes of the crisis. And six projects are being pursued by Fordham faculty in the fields of economics, business, psychology, law, history, and theology.

The book's framework and argument have also been influenced by my experience of teaching a Fordham undergraduate theology course entitled Church in Controversy, in which we explore a variety of church controversies and crises, including the clergy sexual abuse of minors.

Many thanks to my editor, Nancy de Flon, and the team of experts at Paulist Press, who have been immensely helpful during this difficult year. I am especially grateful to Catherine Osborne for her editorial advice, to Galina Krasskova for formatting revisions, and as always, to Christine for her expert line editing. Two chapters benefited from close scrutiny and honest criticisms by writing companions Teresa Delgado, Jeannine Hill Fletcher, Elena Procario Foley, Roger Haight, Paul Lakeland, Michele Saracino, and John Thiel. I've been supported by the friendship of John Seitz, Brenna Moore, Natalia Imperatori-Lee, and Michael Lee, who inspire me by the ways each of them models scholarship that attends closely to struggling individuals and communities. My best friend for many decades, George Didier, has been a regular conversation partner and reality check on all matters psychological.

As I have worked on this difficult subject matter, especially during the time of the coronavirus, I have been particularly grateful for the bonds of love I share with Christine and our sons, Paul and Karl, and their partners, Gabrielle and Jeff.

Chapter 1

Begin with the Laments of the Wounded

The recent terrible history of clergy sex abuse in the United States involves various groups of people. Any way you tell the story, the lives of many characters are interwoven. The main agents—protagonists, but certainly not heroes—are abusive Roman Catholic priests. Their actions and ways of life, as the sex abuse scandal has revealed, sometimes combine horribly vicious deeds with pastoral and charitable activities that gain them reputations for goodness and even holiness. These priest-perpetrators cannot be understood unless we consider them in terms of their seminary formation with other priests-to-be, with the people they serve in parishes, schools, and countless other settings, and in relation to their bishops. The bishop-priest relationship is, in theory, a special one: it combines the roles of father and son, spiritual guide and disciple, and employer and employee. As such, bishops have enormous influence over the lives of the priests in their dioceses. We also cannot consider the priest, the people he serves, and the bishop he is accountable to, without coming to terms with the relationship of his bishop to other bishops in the United States and around the world. This includes, most influentially, the Bishop of Rome, whom Roman Catholics recognize as the pope, the Holy Father, a symbolic source of unity who also exercises central authority in the church. Together this combination of characters constitutes a web of relationships that functions in the church as a global network and a matrix of power.

Yet this chapter will not focus on these clerical characters. Instead, it will concentrate on those who have suffered the most from clergy sex abuse. This first chapter is devoted to heeding the laments of victims, many of whom are also self-identified survivors and some who, tragically, have not survived. Without downplaying the experiences of adults (clergy, nuns, and lay) who have also been the targets of clerical abusers, here we give primary attention to maltreated children and young people. By drawing on their own words and fragments from their stories, we seek to understand varied dimensions of their experiences, constructing a collective portrait of the kinds of victim-survivors involved based on information provided in eight grand jury reports issued between 2001 and 2018. What follows provides both narratives and statistical accounts of who these victims are and also mentions subjects on which we do not yet have sufficient data to offer narrative portraits. We will then ask what interdisciplinary research on trauma teaches us about how to hear and understand these testimonies more deeply. The chapter will conclude by considering theological voices who urge us to heed the testimonies of the traumatized not only in this but in other controversies, arguing that in them we can hear God's Spirit saying something important to us.

This is a chapter about those who have been victimized. But for "us"—myself, and those of you, my readers, who are not victims yourselves—the questions that this chapter will hopefully raise are the following:

- How can we heed the laments of the victims who wish to be recognized as survivors?
- How can we dispose ourselves to be affected by their grieving and outrage?
- What can we learn about how they have been violated and how church cultures and systems have made crimes against these young people possible?
- How can we join these victim-survivors as they wrestle with the traumatic aftermath of their

experiences, and how can we join them in solidarity and accompaniment as they struggle to find a way forward, perhaps by acts of resistance, protest, and calls for radical change in the church?

- How can readers be challenged to change their lives based on this tragic history?

These are hard questions, and for many, reading this chapter will be a hard task. But there is no more important way to understand the clerical sexual abuse crisis. So, let us begin.

A Narrative Portrait of Violations

This testimony was delivered by a woman on February 22, 2019, at a special assembly of the presidents of conferences of bishops from around the world convened in the Vatican.

I wanted to tell you about when I was a child. But there's no point, because when I was 11 years old, a priest from my parish destroyed my life. Since then I, who loved coloring books and doing somersaults on the grass, have not existed.

Instead, engraved in my eyes, ears, nose, body, and soul, are all the times he immobilized me, the child, with superhuman strength: I desensitized myself, I held my breath, I came out of my body, I searched desperately for a window to look out of, waiting for it all to end. I thought: "If I don't move, maybe I won't feel anything; if I don't breathe, maybe I could die."

When it did end, I would take back what was my wounded and humiliated body, and I would leave, even believing I had imagined it all. But how could I, a child, understand what had happened? I thought: "It must have been my fault!" or "Maybe I deserved this bad thing?"

These thoughts are the worst wounds that the abuse, and the abuser, insinuates into your heart, more than the wounds that lacerate your body. I felt I wasn't worth anything anymore. I felt I didn't even exist. I just wanted to die. I tried to...but I couldn't.

The abuse went on for 5 years. No one noticed.

While I did not speak, my body did: eating disorders, various periods in hospital: everything screamed that I was sick. While I, completely alone, kept my pain to myself. They thought I was anxious about school where, suddenly, I was performing really badly.[1]

In the face of such agonizing testimonies, *laments* provide one way to diagnose pivotal dimensions of the phenomenon of clergy sex abuse. This biblical genre has a number of key features. The lament surfaces two profound questions that echo the pleas of minors abused by clergy: Why is this happening to me? How long is this going to go on?

As scholars have discovered, laments often have the deep structure of a trial in which the self, the enemy, and even God are indicted and interrogated. This method and structure can be reflected in the thoughts of people who have been victimized and violated for different reasons. On the one hand, victims question themselves about the reasons for their abuse. Was it something I did? How did I get myself into this situation? Why has the aggressor chosen to harm me? But the transgressor is also on trial in the imagination and feelings of the one who laments; even though a child is rarely able to conceptualize a situation in which the abuser will officially be put on trial, either with superiors, in a court of law, or before God. Why are you, a person I once trusted, doing this? How can you justify this to yourself? By whom and how will you be held accountable for it?

It is not hard to believe that some victims also wish to place God on trial. Why are you, God, letting this happen to me? What is this priestly representative and mediator showing me about God's identity and desires for my life through this behavior? Abusers sometimes insinuate that the victim will get into trouble for performing sexual acts if they inform teachers, parents, or other priests. However, some victims might believe that not only the perpetrator but also God must bear responsibility for this violation and that both God and his agent should suffer the consequences of this crime. On the other hand, the victim might draw the conclusion that God is not protecting the victim and perhaps this situation of horror reveals that there is no God.

What kinds of evidence might be presented at these trials?

Enticements

Mark was only nine when he first met Father X, a parochial vicar at St. Andrew Church in Newtown (Pennsylvania). Father X became a family "friend" who often visited the house. Mark, though, was the subject of special attention from the priest, who persistently wrestled with the boy, rubbed his back and shoulders, and openly brought up sex talk.[2]

Priest-predators employ various forms of enticements identified as "grooming" techniques by experts in the field of abusive behavior.[3] Food, alcohol, games, or just extra attention might become lures. The child may believe that the priest offering these enticements is just taking an interest in him or her, kidding around, or showing care. Typically, such a child's pattern of life intersects with the orbit of a priest's: as an altar server at Mass, a student in class, a scout, or in sports or theater. The young person recognizes that the priest has a respected role in these contexts. In addition, the priest may often socialize with and befriend the child's family, parents (in some cases a single mother) or sisters or brothers.

The child who receives this kind of notice initially feels special and appreciated by a person not only highly regarded in the community but valorized in the church as someone close to God. The child may find the priest's extra attention unusual, yet not unwelcome. But the child may also become uncomfortable with the priest's special interest in her or him and, in some cases, the family's special relationship with the priest. It's a strange feeling, being special to this adult who acts like a friend by playing games, sports, joking around or wrestling, showing the child a good time by taking them out for ice cream or a meal and, as time progresses, to a movie or a sporting event.

If the child is quite young, and especially if the grooming involves the child's family, these initial overtures may evolve into the priest reading to the child or bathing the child in preparation for bed. For older children, things may escalate to touching during liturgical, theatrical, or sports practices. This kind of physical intimacy sets up the contexts and conditions for more invasive behavior by the priest. This behavior can escalate into invitations to stay overnight at the rectory, or to go on a trip to another city or perhaps on a camping venture with other Cub Scouts or Boy Scouts.

Sexual Assault

When Mark was 14, in 1996, Father X was finally ready to make his move. He arranged with Mark's mother for a "sleepover" at an apartment the priest was renting. Once he had the boy there, X showed him pornographic pictures on his computer, bragged about his penis size, and insisted that Mark sleep together with him in his bed. Then he lay down behind the boy and put his penis into the boy's buttocks. Mark told his parents what happened, and they confronted X, but he denied it and they believed the priest. From that point, Mark suffered depression, dramatic weight loss, and drug and alcohol addiction. Ultimately, he attempted suicide. (Philadelphia Grand Jury, 3)

At some point, sooner or later, this pattern of behavior includes physical sexual attention. Taking care of the robes and garments for altar servers, or a physical expression of playing around and wrestling, deteriorates into an incident: a transgression of sexual boundaries in the sacristy, or rectory, or school, or while camping. In some cases, there is drinking, or drugs, or pornography involved. Initiated by the priest, the sexual act itself of whatever kind is likely something the child has never experienced before. In the sacristy or the school, in the parish rectory or the priest's residence, the priest uses the child as a source of psychological and physical gratification, resulting in the priest's or (if a boy) child's erection and, in some instances, penetration and ejaculation. The priest touches the child's body—thigh, backside, and a boy's testicles and penis, or a girl's breasts and vagina—or the priest asks that the child engage in this kind of touching activity with the priest.

In an encounter that might include manual, oral, anal, or vaginal sex, the priest experiences excitement and pleasure, while the child experiences bewilderment, anxiety, fear, confusion, and distress. Depending on what happens, both boys and girls may experience sexual stimulation or pressure and pain, any of which is a further source of agitation. If a boy ejaculates, this compounds the trauma of the experience. The child's experience combines profound physical and psychological displeasure and distress and intense confusion, including the questions already mentioned as the core of laments. Why has the priest done this? Why to *me*? And why *him*, the honored character in the community, the person identified with God and as an agent of God?

Toward the end of the encounter, the priest will usually provide some reason why the child should not speak of this to anyone else: friend, parent, teacher, or another priest. The rationale often entails a very distorted view of the meaning of what has happened and a threat about how there will be very bad consequences if the events are discussed with others.

Aftermath

John started to be abused by a priest when he was 10 and ended up with possibly more than 100 violations, which went through different stages. As he described in an interview, it started with "touching and rubbing" and progressed with "fondling, oral sex, and then anal rape...." After he was 11 years old, he began acting out—"starting fights in school, drinking, coming home late—hoping that someone would notice, that someone would care." "I couldn't understand why my parents didn't help me....And [they] were kind of happy that I was spending time with a priest, ya know—like he'd be the one to straighten me out." As described in the York Daily Record, "His breaking point was at 13. An argument after detention led to him telling his parents what [the priest-abuser] was doing to him...for years. His parents didn't believe him. They asked his abuser to counsel him....He felt trapped,... manipulated,...alone, and isolated."

John Delaney, interview, August 30, 2018[4]

After a priest's violation, the child's relationships with family and peers become strained and at risk. The child is often afraid of speaking to his or her parents about the initial episode and usually any subsequent ones. The priest reiterates why the young person should not tell an adult or peer. If a child does speak up, some parents refuse to believe that the priest could have done such a thing. In certain cases, this results in profound alienation between the child and the parent. If peers find out, they might ostracize and deride the victim.

A child's relationship with God, if the young person was conscious of one before these transgressions occurred, is likely to be shattered by these events. Any sense of being cared for by God is shaken. Since, for a child brought up in a Catholic context, the priest is often identified as a special representative of God, such a sequence of events can call into question many governing assumptions about how God operates. How could this person, honored as holy and beyond reproach in the community, have been the cause of so much pain?

Ongoing Assaults

As the previous testimony of John Delaney indicates, in cases where there is an escalation of attention by the priest and continuing assaults, the results often include deepening introspection and further alienation from parents, family, and peers. Sexual exploitation of a child for any period of time—whether one occasion, several, or over weeks, months, or years—can result in severe physical and psychological damage. This can be manifested in many different ways, including depression, isolation, self-abusive behavior, and, in numerous cases, suicide attempts.

8

There is invariably a loss of innocence. Being abused by a priest deprives a young person of their own decision-making process regarding sexuality. Victims are robbed of the experiences of the joys and difficulties and ambiguities of sexual encounters as young people. The cloud of violation, and, with it, feelings of displaced anger, aggression, and depression, will often be associated with sexual relationships as they get older.

Telling an Adult What Happened

As mentioned, in most cases the abuser has warned and even threatened the young person against talking to an adult about what is happening—whether to the pastor or another priest, a parent, a teacher, or anyone else in authority. Depending on the psychological constitution of the abused youth, there may be a great deal of apprehension and possibly paranoia about speaking to anyone about the abuse. If the young person does speak to an adult, that adult will, optimally, be empathetic, receptive, and protective. He or she will express anger toward the transgressor for his criminal offense. And the adult will communicate without reservation that he or she takes the abused person's point of view and side in this struggle.

Yet not every young person who does decide to speak out finds this kind of receptive adult listener. Instead, they might encounter what can only be called a second form of maltreatment by an adult, a violation that is not sexual, but still a transgression that inflicts further wounds. In many cases the adult to whom a child confides equivocates and vacillates about whether to believe the young person or not. Sometimes a parent denies their child's testimony and even, though in relatively unusual cases, reacts with anger, rage, and violence toward the child, asking, "How could you be saying this about a priest, or about this priest?"[5]

Compounding Trauma: A Second Violation

When an adult representative of the church has been told about the violation, in many cases the bishop, or the clergy assigned to speak on behalf of the bishop, never followed up to meet and talk with the abused person or with their parents. In fact, for decades, when official representatives of the church were informed about such violations, they primarily devoted their attention to the priests —their protection, their mental health, or their reassignment— and not to the abused child. The lack of attention to the abused child once the incident has been brought to light leaves the young person and their adult caregivers feeling disregarded and disrespected.

Far too often, an additional form of violation and indeed crime occurred after a representative of the church listened to victims' testimony. Between 1950 and 2002, dioceses regularly worked with lawyers to determine whether the account was credible, how damaged the young person was by the priest's behavior, and how much money should be provided to the parents in compensation and to cover the expense of counseling. Many maintain that victims and their caregivers did not receive the kind of financial settlement warranted by this kind of crime. Moreover, the diocesan office responsible for assigning priests to their next parish appointments often sent perpetrators for psychological counseling, and then moved them to another assignment where they continued to have contact with minor children. This series of actions added insult to the original injury, not to mention putting many additional children at risk. The net effect was that criminal behavior was concealed in order to avoid adversely affecting the reputation of the church and draining its financial resources, both of which could have called into question the institution's future viability. For victim-survivors and their families, this second form of maltreatment, or second act of violation, contributed to a new level of woundedness and a profound sense of betrayal. As the church protected itself, the children who had been victimized were left on their own to deal with the suffering, which is described in the Philadelphia Grand Jury Report:

> Billy (pseudonym) felt as though he had lost himself—or the person he used to be—as a result of Fr. X's abuse. He described what the priest had done as "turn[ing] this

good kid into this monster." He began to think of himself as two different people. He told the Jurors:

I had no God to turn to, no family, and it just went from having one person in me to having two people inside me.

This nice [Billy] that used to live, and then this evil, this darkness [Billy] that had to have no morals and no conscience in order to get by day by day and, you know, not to care about anything or have no feelings and to bury th[ose] feelings so that you could live every day and not be laying on the couch with a depression problem so bad that, you know, four days later you'd be in the same spot.[6]

A Statistical Portrait

The statistical findings presented here were gathered and analyzed by the John Jay College of Criminal Justice between March 2003 and February 2004. Of the 202 dioceses and 221 religious orders of men the researchers contacted, 195 dioceses and 140 religious institutes responded. This latter number constitutes roughly 60 percent of such communities but about 80 percent of priests in these communities (2004, 3, 13). Based on this data, the John Jay Report calculated a total number of 10,667 children who were victims of sexual transgression between 1950, which represents the first year when cases of clergy sex abuse of minors were recorded, and 2002, the year when this phase of the investigation came to an end (2004, 69). More recent statistics will receive attention later in this section.

Researchers note, however, that victims of sex abuse underreport, including for some of the reasons suggested in the last section. Perhaps "a third of female victims and a greater percentage of male victims never disclose their violations to anyone."[7] According to the John Jay Report, "1,176 incidents, or slightly more than one in ten, were reported quickly. In contrast, 41%...were reported after more than 25 years."[8] Moreover, many dioceses and religious orders did not keep accurate records, nor did all dioceses contribute information to the John Jay investigation. Thus, clinical psychologist Mary Gail Frawley-O'Dea judges, "It is...reasonable to estimate that over fifty thousand young people were abused by priests over the fifty years encompassed by the study."[9]

Of those dioceses in the John Jay study who reported the gender of the victims, 80.9 percent were male (8,499) and 19.1 percent were female (2,004); but the percentage of female victims noticeably increased after 1994, when girls were first allowed to become altar servers.[10] Over 50 percent of victims were between the ages 11 and 14, 27.3 percent were between 15 and 17, 16 percent between 8 and 10, and 6 percent under the age of 7.[11] "Over 40% of all victims were males between the ages of 11 and 14" (2004, 6).

The John Jay Report concentrated on the data they received about the accused clergy and did not ask research questions about what percentage of the affected minors were from economically disadvantaged or working-class families. The report did observe that some of the victims were from divorced families or had single parents. Since 2018 noticeably more victims from people of color—Native American, Latin American, and Black communities—have received attention, but none of these groups of abused was identified in the 2004 John Jay Report because the dioceses provided none of this information.

The 2004 study identified the most common form of grooming behavior by priest-abusers. Young people were often enticed with alcohol or drugs (712 instances, 38.8%). There was also a large number of incidents of the youth staying overnight with the priest in the rectory (559, 30.5%) or taken to sports or recreational events (427, 23.3%). In some cases, the priest gave the victim money (377, 20.6%). Other forms of enticement included a priest forming a relationship with a family, which provided a context for the priest to express an interest, caring, and increasing closeness with the parent's son or daughter or a number of the children.

The report delineated a variety of ways the priest can violate the young person, by exercising power in physical and sexual ways, but also through verbal and spiritual forms of manipulation. Priests most often violated the sexual integrity of the youth by touching them over their clothes (52.6%), or under their clothes (44.9%), whether male or female. The clergy performed oral sex on the victim in 26 percent of incidents, and the victim performed oral sex on the priest in 14.2 percent of incidents. In 11.8 percent of incidents, the priest undressed, and slightly more often (14.9%) the victim reports having undressed. In the only kinds of incident technically defined as rape, the priest engaged in manual penetration with female victims (10.9%) and penile penetration with male youth (12.9%) and female youth (11.9%).[12] Commonly, the abuser engages in more than one form of transgressive sexual behavior with the victim (2004, 73). In 2,759 cases (about 29%) it was reported that the alleged abusive behavior occurred only once, but some report that it occurred more than once (1,734, 18.3%) while over 50 percent said it occurred numerous times (5,002, 52.7%) (2004, 74).

Two years after the original John Jay Report was released, a follow-up study was issued that considered whether any variables shed light on why there is a gap of time, sometimes decades, before victims come forward to report the incident. One obvious possibility would be that many victims chose to come forward following other major revelations about clergy sex abuse reported on television and in print media. The most notorious of these cases were Gilbert Gauthe in Louisiana in 1984; James Porter in Fall River, Massachusetts in 1992; John Geoghan from Boston, who was prosecuted in 1991 for serial molestation; Rudy Kos from Texas in 1998; and then the *Boston Globe* Spotlight investigation reports, which began on January 2, 2002. These incidents all certainly contributed to increased numbers of victims coming forward to report being abused, as did the ten grand jury reports (2002–18) from East Coast states identifying the names of credibly accused priests and the allegations against them.[13] The John Jay Supplemental Report also proposed that reporting abuse could be substantially delayed if the contacts between the abuser and the victim were more frequent, the contacts went on for a longer period of time, if the sexual acts were more severe, or if any combination of these conditions obtained (2006, 10).

Some new streams of information about clergy sex abuse of minors have also been made public since the John Jay Reports' release in 2004, 2006, and 2012. It may be best to keep in mind

Frawley-O'Dea's educated guess that over 50,000 young people were abused, in comparison with the number of 10,667 individuals mentioned in the John Jay Reports. The August 28, 2018, report of the Center for Applied Research in the Apostolate (CARA) at Georgetown University indicated that between 2004 and 2017, there were 8,694 new allegations, which gives us a total count of 19,336 allegations, and 22 allegations after that report, resulting in a total of 19,358.[14]

Gaps in the Portraits:
What Don't We Know Yet?

Numerous evaluations of the John Jay Report, some of them quite critical, have been published.[15] It was inevitable that there would be limitations in this multivolume report, and the research cannot on its face be charged with intentional deception. The researchers could only provide a statistical portrait based on the information they received from the bishops. There are people who believe that the document was tainted due to its being funded by the U.S. Bishops' Conference and commissioned by one of its subsidiary organizations, the National Review Board. And, as mentioned, John Jay researchers did not receive data from every diocese and religious institute in the United States.

Moreover, as also mentioned, the dioceses did not provide information about the socioeconomic status of the victims. There is no information about the racial and ethnic composition of the victims in the records provided by the bishops. There is also no consideration of the church's role in the ongoing legacy of racism, colonialism, and neocolonialism among people of color as it bears upon clergy sex abuse. As a result, the John Jay Report could not address the church's policy of silence on these dimensions of the scandal.

The statistical findings of the John Jay Report, combined with the results of work of the Center for Applied Research in the Apostolate (CARA), are based on initial data supplied by the bishops. In addition, inconsistently and sometimes with questionable motives, the bishops of a number of dioceses and the superiors of some religious orders have released lists of priests and brothers who have been accused and convicted of sexually abusing minors. Again, these reports contain no information about the victims, and there are diverse levels of reporting about the cities, parishes, and schools where the accused and convicted priests provided their ministry and during what time periods. None of these sources provides any data about the socioeconomic, racial, ethnic, and Indigenous identities of victims.

These gaps in the statistical and historical narratives are being addressed in a fresh wave of research and articles published by scholars working on Indigenous populations and by cultural historians examining archival materials and interviewing victim-survivors. As in the earlier wave of research, media reports have also assisted here; for example, news organizations have relatively recently examined the differential treatment of Black victims in Mississippi and Indigenous victims in Western Alaska.[16] Wider studies are being conducted on instances of abuse in communities suffering from the ongoing problems of settler colonialism,[17] and there is promise of new publications exploring the lives of victims and their efforts to deal with the consequences of clergy sex abuse in their subsequent lives.[18]

A Deeper Pedagogy: What Trauma Theory Teaches

Considerable attention has been given to the study of trauma in situations of sexual abuse, including with minors, as well as trauma experienced in conditions of war, terrorism, and organized crime. This research has informed theories in psychology, medicine, and psychoanalysis that attempt to understand and explain situations of violent sexual trauma and also to advance therapies to assist victims struggling with the resulting wounds and dysfunctions. Three key discoveries from this trauma research, introduced here, can aid us in gaining deeper insight into the laments of clergy sex abuse victims. Moreover, they will help us appreciate why listening to victims will better enable us, personally and collectively, to grasp and to respond to the wounds inflicted and to the personal and institutional dysfunctions that facilitate these destructive clerical behaviors.

The first and most important feature of trauma identified by psychologists and psychoanalysts is the phenomenon called *dissociation*. In the words of Bessel van der Kolk, "dissociation is the essence of trauma. The overwhelming experience is split off and fragmented, so that the emotions, sounds, images, thoughts, and physical sensation related to the trauma take on a life of their own."[19] Judith Herman describes the phenomenon in this way: "The conflict between the will to deny horrible events and the will to proclaim them aloud is the central dialectic of psychological trauma....Dissociation results in the protean, dramatic, and often bizarre symptoms of hysteria which Freud recognized a century ago as disguised communication about sexual abuse in childhood."[20]

Therapists report that the laments and groans of clergy sex abuse victims often encompass disconnected, strange speech conveying confusing messages. There are many instances of loss or fragmentation of memories about experiences of abuse, and sometimes even years later there is an inability to narrate the sequence of this part of one's personal history and difficulty expressing the myriad feelings elicited by the abuse. As the testimony of "Billy" cited above reflects, these victims shoulder feelings of guilt and shame, confusion and numbness, which are often combined with feelings of fear, anger, aggression, as well as helplessness and depression.

This cacophony of emotions can result in self-berating and self-wounding, and a desire to harm oneself, including, for some people, to consider suicidal urges. In many cases a victim who is a minor cannot consciously acknowledge and recall, sometimes for ten or twenty or more years, what has taken place in traumatic sexual occurrences. Their minds and bodies set up obstacles to facing what has happened, and the victim can perceive a spectrum of emotions, sounds, smells, and bodily pain that seem split off, resulting in a deeply divided and fragmented sense of self. Victims' laments express this range of affects and the fundamental vulnerability involved. These manifestations of clergy abuse in the psyche of the child and the teenager can continue for months and often for years into adulthood. The personal damage of this abuse is a heavy weight to carry. Signs of a dissociative mind are not only associated with this combination of feelings but are also often revealed in the body—stomach disorders, high blood pressure, insomnia, and alcohol or drug dependency. This explains Van der Kolk's refrain: "the body keeps the score."

A second feature of sexual trauma that has particular relevance in a consideration of clergy sex abuse of minors pertains to the betrayal of victims by a trusted person representing a respected institution and community. Trauma theorists often describe this as a second form of abuse. In cases of clergy sex abuse, church officials such as bishops and their official representatives, or provincials of religious orders such as Jesuits, Dominicans, and Franciscans, have too often not listened fully to the victims, have undermined their testimony, and have not followed through appropriately on their complaints. By what they say and do, or what they do *not* say and do, authority figures such as these "effectively take the side of the perpetrators in their midst."[21] Church authorities and representatives, as mentioned, primarily sought to protect the reputation of the institution as pure, credible, and reliable by employing secrecy and cover-up and failed to take action to protect children from being damaged or at risk. They also often actively protected the accused priest by moving him to a new parish, not reporting him to legal authorities, and minimizing the severity of the offense. But as Herman expresses it,

> What seems of paramount importance to most survivors is social validation—that is, public acknowledgement of both the effects and the harms of this crime. Beyond this, what survivors desire most is vindication; they want their communities to take a clear stand in denouncing the crime so that the burdens of shame are lifted from their shoulders and placed on the offenders, where they rightfully belong.[22]

A third lesson learned from therapists and critical theories is that the victims of sex abuse experience serious "subjugation of the self" after being overpowered sexually, physically, psychologically, and by means of authority structures and religious practices. These wounded and vulnerable people often are left to struggle, sometimes throughout their lives, in order to advance what has been designated "subject formation," which requires an internal struggle against the legacy of subjugation by exercising human agency through resistance and by discovering, reclaiming, and to a certain extent creating a stable sense of their own self-identity. In cases of clergy sex abuse there is often a double defeat of the self, by the priest-abuser and through the institutional betrayal by means of secrecy and cover-up. Victims' healing, which we might hope for through some integration of the dissociated self and a reconciliation of the betrayed self with the community, are not always attainable or only emerge in fits and starts. Yet, these forms of subjugation create areas of conflict and struggle through which self-formation and self-realization can take place, even in cases where defeat may be compounded. Out of this crucible, this cauldron, a formation of the self can take place, but usually not without the assistance of professionals, loved ones, or fellow advocates for change, whether outside of, at the margins of, or within the church. Clergy sex abuse is an extreme form of the traumatic destruction of the self-examined by psychologists, but it provides a clear instance of how actualizing the self in the wake of such events requires opposition—contesting, resisting, and subversion—through self-formation. In certain instances, this process can provide the conditions for victim-survivors to confront dysfunctions in the church or other social institutions.

The Groaning of God's Spirit in the Wounded

When theologians and those initiated into the Christian faith ponder the laments of traumatized victims, it is customary, and one could say traditional, for believers to wrestle with these experiences in terms of biblical and liturgical witnesses to Jesus Christ, who is professed to be a prophetic figure who has been crucified for what he said and did but is also honored and worshiped by Christians as the one who heeds, receives, and embodies the Word of God made flesh. When Christians reflect upon the laments of victims, Jesus Christ crucified, the Word made flesh, is often the center of their devotions.

It is widely recognized, and increasingly so, that there are also venerable scriptural teachings and doctrinal and liturgical traditions that also offer narrative testimonies to the voice of the Spirit of God heeded, received, and responded to in the laments of humans and even in the cries of the damaged earth, sometimes in moaning and groans that are difficult to understand. Jesus's own sense of mission in the Gospels is attributed to his responsiveness to the voice of the Spirit of God in the poor, the marginalized, and the traumatized.

Through baptism Christians are called upon and anointed by the Spirit of God to participate in the prophetic charism and office of Jesus Christ through a life of missionary discipleship to exercise a *prophetic obedience of faith* by heeding, receiving, and responding to the voice of the Spirit of God as well as to the word of God in the Scriptures and tradition. And in cases such as clergy sex abuse, Christian faith can instruct those who are receptive that the voice of the Spirit can be perceived in the laments and aspirations of those with wounded bodies and spirits, and those suffering within dysfunctional communities and institutions. We need the twofold dimensions of the prophetic office of Jesus Christ, who heeds, receives, and responds to the voice of the Spirit in laments, and who heeds, receives, and responds to the Word of God and becomes the Word of God in human form. Both dimensions of prophetic obedience are needed in order to recognize and heed God's Spirit speaking from within the "sense of the faith" of all the people of God.

Let us consider how this concentration on Jesus Christ crucified and on the Spirit of God is being expressed in contemporary theologians' reflections on trauma in other areas of our recent history. Following World War II, a small group of Christians and theologians were devastated by the complicity of many Christians in the horror called the Shoah, Nazi Germany's mass murder of Jews. Protestant and Catholic theologians approached this trauma by meditating on the crucifixion. German Protestant theologian Jürgen Moltmann called upon Christians to profess Jesus Christ as the Crucified God who suffers with victims, in light of this Christian shame. German Catholic theologian Johann Baptist Metz in a similar manner reflected on the "dangerous memory" of the Shoah in relation to the *memoria passionis et resurrectionis Jesus Christi*—the memory of the suffering and resurrection of Jesus Christ. For Metz, a memory becomes dangerous when, among other things, it impels people in the present to understand and act against a sinful status quo.[23] The cross and resurrection of Christ have been invoked by believers in countless other tragedies in recent world history.

In another instance, during the civil war in El Salvador (1979–92), theologians Oscar Romero, Ignacio Ellacuría, and Jon Sobrino focused attention on the country's suffering poor by identifying them as a crucified people and as collective victims of the violence evoked in the song of the Suffering Servant of God (Isa 42). These leaders called on the church to take this crucified people down from the cross rather than supporting their torturers.[24]

Jesus Christ crucified also has been a central symbol in the long and ongoing traumatic history of African Americans struggling with the legacy of slavery, racism, and colonialism. James Cone, the founder of contemporary Black theology, often wrote about racism in relation to Christ crucified, and in the waning years of his life he wrote *The Cross and the Lynching Tree*, a meditation on the horrible analogies between the two real historical events of crucifixion and lynching and their conjoined theological meanings.

Black Catholic theologian M. Shawn Copeland has made an important intervention on the trauma of racism by engaging in deep reflection on the role of the body of Christ and the embodiment of slavery as well as many forms of racism and white supremacy and white privilege. Copeland begins her book *Enfleshing Freedom* with a quote from the prophet Jeremiah: "The wounds of my people wound me too. Is there no balm in Gilead? Who will turn my head into a fountain and my eyes into a spring of tears so that I may weep all day, all night for the wounded out of my people?"[25] Her extended argument culminates with a meditation on the scarred and mutilated Black bodies that have suffered as a consequence of racism, which evoke the "memory of the scarred body of the Risen Christ" that Thomas encounters when the "Lord of Life seals his identity with the crucified Jesus of Nazareth by displaying his wounds." Copeland invite her readers to discover that the "broken body communicates the risk of enfleshing freedom.... The marks on her flesh identify her, tell us who she is, and bear witness to her desire and agency."[26] Copeland's resolutely christocentric approach finds its capstone in eucharistic solidarity. For her, the dangerous memory of the wounded Jesus Christ now risen is celebrated in the assembly of the Body of Christ, which becomes what it receives in the Eucharist through the social consequences realized through praxis.[27]

Several feminist theologians, both Catholic and Protestant, have recently mined the interdisciplinary insights to be gained from reflection on all forms of trauma. Jennifer Beste and Erin Kidd have both focused on trauma victims' bodies (corporeality), the phenomenon of precariousness, and grief. Beste and Kidd are particularly interested in the formation of the self in relation to experiences of trauma, especially in terms of the power of freedom and the efficacy of God's grace.[28]

Serene Jones, meanwhile, in her widely read book *Trauma and Grace*, investigates the myriad ways traumatic events wound the self by disordering the imagination, the memory, and the use of language and speech, and lifts up the resources that the Christian gospel can provide for reordering and healing the imagination.[29] Like Copeland's, Jones's approach is christocentric, as, centering on the cross of Christ, she describes the crucified imaginings of alluring, mirroring, and unending (69–98) as resources for struggling with traumatic experiences. She also provides valuable reflections on the power of grace as it may be encountered in redeeming ruptures that can occur amid the difficulties confronted in different forms of trauma.

Jones's engagement with trauma in relation to John Calvin's *Commentary on the Book of Psalms*, which she sees as providing an anatomy of the soul and a healing performance of prayer, intersects fruitfully with my own approach to the importance of the genre of lamentations in the Psalms. Jones invokes Judith Herman's delineation of three stages in the healing of traumatized people: "The central task of the first stage is the establishment of safety. The central task of the second stage is remembrance and mourning. The central task of the third stage is reconnection with ordinary life."[30] Jones perceives these three stages as comparable to John Calvin's tripartite division of the types of psalms: deliverance, lamentations, and thanksgiving. Her insightful comparison of Herman's three stages with Calvin's three species of psalms offers a platform for a compelling argument about the importance of these three forms of psalms in contributing to an anatomy of the soul and about their healing role in the performance of prayer. While acknowledging this tripartite division, I will accentuate below certain insights lamentations provide for recognizing the voice of the Spirit in voices of traumatized victims and in the groans and wails in the depths of darkness and opacity encountered in trauma.

At this point my argument converges more closely with and is enriched by Bryan Massingale's treatment of laments amid experiences of racial injustice in the church and in civil society.[31] I see Massingale's treatment of lament as conceptually interrelated with his expressed exasperation at the failure of Catholic bishops, clergy, and laity to address issues of racism and at their timidity about expressing prophetic anger in face of racial injustice. For Massingale personally, and likely many in the Black Catholic community, this failure contributes to a contemporary spiritual experience of the dark night of the soul among many in the Black community and their allies, where a felt absence of God and the presence of racism contribute to spiritual desolation. Multigenerational manifestations of racism and its economic and cultural repercussions are deeply wounding and, in many cases, literally death-dealing for African Americans and other people of color in the United States, for whom they constitute a situation of ongoing, chronic trauma. Although Massingale does not connect his line of argument with the voice and agency of the Spirit of God at work in the laments, resistance, and protest of clergy sex abuse victims, to do so would be entirely consistent. Here is another traumatic site of wounding, pathology, and dysfunction in the church and in civil society that needs the diagnosis gained by the sense of the faithful who testify to the voice of the Spirit in the depths of their laments.

More so than her theological contemporaries, Shelly Rambo's 2010 book, *Spirit and Trauma: A Theology of Remaining*, devotes extensive attention to the role of the Spirit in traumatic experiences.[32] Rambo's great contribution is in mapping the working of what she speaks of as the "middle Spirit," drawing on themes from the renowned theologian Hans Urs von Balthasar's explication of the great mystery of Easter.[33] In the movement between the crucified and the resurrected Lord between Good Friday and Easter, in the darkness of the netherworld in Jesus's descent into hell on Holy Saturday as confessed in the Apostles' Creed, Rambo seeks to plumb insights for those who have undergone trauma. She considers these dark spaces in terms of the theme of "remaining" prominent in John's Gospel. The middle Spirit, she proposes, enables one to move in and between the difficult spaces of past traumatic events and the now, where language and memory and imagination can be fractured and fragmented and can betray, but can also be healed and restored.

Conclusion

This chapter has attempted to engage in critical listening with those who have been traumatized by clergy sex abuse in order to understand the nature and extent of their wounds and to gain insights from these victims about the forms and roles played in their suffering by pathology and dysfunctions in the church. What do we learn about the church in controversy from those who have been, first, sexually abused by priests and, second, also abused by having their dignity, views, and insights ignored or disrespected by the institutional church? If we listen to these victims, and indeed to all of those who grieve due to other sources of trauma in the church, what might we learn? Consider, for instance, the women, both women religious and laywomen, who have been prohibited from serving as leaders, lay or ordained ministers, or preachers, and from collaborating as equals in exercising leadership in the church. What could we learn from them about how the church is wounded by misogyny? If we who are white Christians would truly listen to the laments of people of color who have been deeply wounded by how they have been violated by the racism and colonialism of the people of God in their parishes and dioceses, what would we learn? What if we compounded these lessons by listening especially to women and racial minorities who have *also* been sexually abused by clergy?

While this book focuses on clergy sex abuse of victims who were minors when their sexual abuse initially began, I argue that these victim-survivors are teaching the universal church, offering crucial insights into how listening to the laments of victims and the abused can provide a way for the Spirit of truth to be heard. In their testimonies I thus perceive a crucial venue through which the sense of the traumatized faithful is being voiced. The church, which has long spoken of "the sense of the faithful," does not tap into believers' lived faith and wisdom by asking what they heed, receive, and respond to in the word of God. This is how we often think about how the lay faithful partake in the prophetic office of Christ. But in the face of the testimony of the traumatized faithful, we need to expand our understanding, to pay attention to the Spirit-impelled ways of "speaking in tongues"—often perceived as distorted speech—by those who have been senselessly abused, and to the wounded wails of people traumatized in the church in countless other ways. Only by so doing can this horrifying history be adequately heeded, received, and responded to by graced actions worthy of the Word and Spirit.

At this point you might want to pause and consider some questions and perhaps discuss them with your reading group. Have you ever witnessed, participated in, or experienced different kinds of trauma in a church or religious community, or in our wider society? Try writing a lament that expresses your own perspective on one of these traumas. The subsequent discussion may or may not include the trauma of clergy sex abuse of minors. Maybe, for you or your peers, there are more common experiences of trauma that have taken place in church, in families, in civil society, or in school. Perhaps some of these have to do with race, gender, or sexual orientation. How do these traumatic experiences give rise to controversies within the church or in society? Where do you hear the Spirit in your own or others' laments?

There is no avoiding laments when dealing with cases of trauma, marginalization, and oppression. The causes and far-ranging effects of abuse and trauma cannot be accurately diagnosed without careful listening to the victims. We must, individually and collectively, cultivate the skills and the theoretical resources to conduct critical incident reporting both with victims and with abusers and the ability to discern the larger systemic dynamics in which their actions are enmeshed. Insufficient listening skills and insufficient theories will result in insufficient diagnosis of the causes and a poor prognosis for attempts to respond.

Chapter 2

The Anatomy of a Pathology

Laments provide opportunities to diagnose the traumas experienced by victims; but they also surface questions about why these
acts occurred in the first place. For our purposes here, this "why"
raises important questions about both the abusive clergy themselves and their enablers within the institutional church. In order
to address these questions, this chapter will analyze the pathology
of clergy sex abuse.

What are the causes of the damaging behavior associated with
clergy sex abuse in the Catholic Church and its concealment? Is it
accurate to say that this behavior indicates a personal pathology,
implying deviant behavior by individuals?[1] Or can pathology also
be used as a metaphor to distinguish destructive patterns of behavior of social groups and institutions such as the Catholic Church?
Whether in the case of individuals or groups, such pathologies
often can encompass a problematic desire, a distorted sense of
duty, or both.[2]

These are opaque areas of human behavior that raise challenging questions, and to probe them requires interdisciplinary
resources, including the tools of critical theories. We know that
clergy abusers' violent actions have wounded individuals, families,
loved ones, and communities. They also reveal cultural and systemic problems and dysfunctions in the church. We are focusing
here on clergy sex abuse of minors, but what is operative in these

cases may also provide a model or a template for analyzing different, sometimes intersecting, controversies in the church and in society that wound people and manifest underlying social pathologies and dysfunctions.

Developing this kind of anatomy of a pathology operative in the church can, in addition, cultivate a certain kind of intelligence, critical insight, and wisdom that, I think, can strengthen our abilities to diagnose similar or even significantly different kinds of wounds and dysfunctions in the church, and by extension, in civil society and social institutions. Along the way, victims and survivors of this and similar types of abuse, trauma, and injustice can become our venerated companions, teachers, and leaders as we consider how to understand these matters, and what must be done to confront them.

This chapter will be divided into two parts. The first part will explore three of the most widely recognized interdisciplinary analyses of clergy sexual abuse of minors: the reports prepared by the John Jay College of Criminal Justice and seminal books by two psychotherapists, Marie Keenan from Ireland and Mary Gail Frawley-O'Dea from the United States. The second half of the chapter will consider how clergy sex abuse and its cover-up have been analyzed within the Catholic Church by Popes John Paul II, Benedict XVI, and Francis primarily in terms of the theological category of sin. The overall aim of the chapter is to foster a wide-angled analysis and assessment of the actions involved in this and other egregious and damaging behaviors in the church.

Interdisciplinary Assessments

John Jay Reports—a Quantitative and Qualitative Reckoning[3]

Six months after the *Boston Globe* Spotlight series of stories on Catholic clergy sex abuse began on January 3, 2002, the United States Catholic Conference of Bishops (USCCB) ratified its new Charter for the Protection of Children and Young People.[4] This

"Dallas Charter" established policies to guarantee a safe environment in Catholic churches and schools and established a "zero tolerance" policy for sexual abuse. It also established a National Review Board (NRB) composed of twelve Catholic laypeople to assist the newly formed Office for Child and Youth Protection and charged it to commission the preparation of an empirically based analysis of the nature and scope of clergy sex abuse of minors and young people in the United States.

The NRB selected a team from the religiously unaffiliated John Jay College of Criminal Justice to conduct research and prepare a report on their findings on clergy abusers and victims between 1950 and 2002. The initial 285-page report, *The Nature and Scope of Sexual Abuse of Minors by Catholic Priests and Deacons, 1950–2002*, was issued in February 2004, with a supplemental report released in February 2006. A third document, *Causes and Context of Sexual Abuse of Minors by Catholic Priests in the United States, 1950–2010*, was released in May 2011.

The objective of this last volume was to situate the causes of the crisis within a historical and cultural frame of reference. That report states on a number of occasions that "no single cause of sexual abuse of minors by Catholic priests is identified as a result of our research" (see, e.g., 2011, 2, 24, 74), and correlatively, that "priests who sexually abused minors constitute a heterogeneous population" (118). Its historical contextualization is one of the great contributions of this 2011 report. Importantly, the research findings discredit certain commonly invoked hypotheses about the primary causes for the crisis. Most noticeably this report rejects the hypothesis that either celibacy (34–35) or homosexuality (36, 74) is the cause of the crisis. This does not mean that these topics are not worthy of further consideration relative to clergy sex abuse. The document likewise discredits the claim that all clergy sex abuse of young people manifests as pedophilia, which is, strictly speaking, associated with abusing multiple young people who are eleven or younger (34–35, 74). The report distinguishes what is technically called "ephebophilia" (the abuse of many young people over the age of eleven) along with the many instances of a single or several acts of abuse by clergy not covered by the previous categories.

Together, the John Jay Reports provide a deep exploration and wide-angle panorama of the crisis drawing on empirical methods, both quantitative and qualitative, with a longitudinal analysis of data gathered from different time periods, surveys, clinical data, and interviews. The third volume, in particular, examines historical and sociocultural factors in U.S. society and seminary education and formation, along with individual-psychological and organizational factors.

Causes and Context builds on the basic historical finding of the first two volumes of the report based on reports of incidents between 1950 and 2002, which are combined in this volume with findings between 2002 and 2010.[5] While incidents of abuse evidently escalated between 1965 and 1985, their reporting to legal and ecclesial officials did not dramatically increase until after 1985, with a second increase beginning in 2001, corresponding to a period of heightened publicity about ecclesial sexual abuse (2011, 118). Though incidents of abuse have never disappeared entirely, by the time the extent of the crisis was being realized by the public, it appeared that the increase in incidents of abuse between 1965 and 1985 was a past historical event that had in large part subsided.

However, the historical effects on victims and the history of their reception were by no means over, and for some they would never be over. Moreover, the growing acknowledgment of what had transpired, brought about by the public testimony of survivors along with the filing of lawsuits, juridical processes, and reports by attorneys general and grand juries—and very belatedly by actions of popes, cardinals, bishops, and priests—resulted in a profound and widely felt sense of betrayal among many in the Catholic Church. And while the crisis of clergy sexual abuse most directly concerns the sexual acts of priest-abusers, both the crisis and the historical problem of clerical sexual abuse are no less about the way bishops and provincials of religious orders of priests have addressed, and continue to address, past patterns of behavior by abuser priests. The scandal of clerical sexual abuse is therefore not over, despite what seems to be a dramatic drop in incidents after the early 1980s.

It is commonly assumed that incidents of sexual abuse of any kind are significantly underreported and are often not disclosed until years or even decades after they occur. Before 1985 only a small percentage of parents reported on their child's abuse within a year; by the mid-1990s there were many more reports of incidents that had occurred ten or more years earlier, and by 2002 the highest percentage of adult victims were reporting on abuse that had taken place twenty to forty years earlier (2011, 118). Finally, the report situates this information about clergy sexual abuse within the broader context of the dramatically growing awareness of the problem of sex abuse in the United States since 1950.

Without diminishing the horrifying character of the incidents of sexual abuse by Catholic clergy, the 2011 report also contextualizes this phenomenon in relation to the broader trends of sexual abuse in the United States, especially in other religious and nonreligious institutions and organizations. The document provides an overview of the sexual abuse of youth in youth-serving organizations—schools, childcare, Boy Scouts of America, Big Brothers and Big Sisters, and athletic organizations. It also discusses abuse in various religious institutions—Christian, Jehovah's Witnesses, Mormon, and Jewish—and within families (2011, 16–24). Catholic clergy's sexual abuse of minors must be understood in terms of a wider-scale phenomenon of the sexual abuse of minors and young people in the United States. Beyond the scope of this report, it is now widely recognized that Catholic clergy's sexual abuse of minors is a global phenomenon, based on reports from Ireland, Australia, Colombia, Germany, and Poland, among others. This data is also being reconsidered in relation to recent revelations about Catholic clergy's sexual abuse of women religious globally, especially in the southern hemisphere.

What is the most important information that the John Jay researchers give us about the sociohistorical context of priests who went on to become abusers? Those clergy at the center of the investigation were ordained between the 1930s and 1950s, with the statistical high point of the actual abuse taking place between 1965 and 1985. The vast majority of priest-abusers (70 percent) were ordained before the 1970s, and most went through seminary either before the Second Vatican Council or before its reforms began to be implemented. Many of the priests engaging in sexually abusive behavior lived during a time of social upheaval in U.S. history associated with the sexual revolution, the burgeoning feminist movement, the civil rights era, the emergence of the gay liberation movement, and the anti–Vietnam War movement. Religious and civil authorities and moral frameworks were being questioned and challenged.

This was a tumultuous time of change in both the United States and the Catholic Church. The Second Vatican Council initiated a period of dramatic reform in the church. While the church officially encouraged more openness to the world and society, and a less rigid, more pastorally engaged approach to priesthood, Pope Paul VI rejected the call to allow the use of birth control in marriage, and later, in the 1980s and through the early 2000s, John Paul II and Benedict XVI banned open discussion in the church about married clergy and the ordination of women. In the midst of an older model of priesthood being questioned and rejected by increasing numbers of clergy and by the laity beginning in the 1960s, seminarians and priests were also confronted with a growing amount of men leaving the priesthood to get married. The pope and, by extension, the teaching office of the church were also unwilling to engage questions being raised about homosexuality in the church and about the phenomenon of openly gay priests, both of which began to become issues in the 1970s and 1980s. Rather than responding in a dialogical spirit to these challenges, the church instead placed an increased emphasis on strict moral requirements and clerical celibacy, promoting a heroic approach to virtue and greater emphasis on "the ontological shift" among ordained priests (2011, 68). This latter refers to the common belief that ordination to the priesthood entails, if not an ascent to superhuman status, a real shift in one's being, such that one is no longer "like" other human beings. Situated within this setting, how, as historian John Seitz asks, do we narrate the emotional history of priests during this tumultuous historical period?[6]

The John Jay Reports try to identify characteristics of priest-abusers, using various forms of psychological analysis to track down the causes of sexual abuse. These included examining results from psychological tests and clinical data about clergy members' families, sexual histories, levels of esteem, social bonding, and self-constructed narratives of priests that reveal their self-understanding.

In examining priests who had engaged in incidents of abuse as well as those who did not, the researchers found this overarching set of conclusions:

> Accused priests did not provide a different narrative structure for their life course than non-accused priests.... They provided similar narratives of coming to the priesthood, whether they were internally motivated by the call of God, or externally nudged in the direction of the priesthood by priests and sisters in the ministry or by other family members or friends....Accused and non-accused priests provided similar narratives about the process of being ordained (experiencing the ontological shift) and how the resolution of coming to the priest role is one of negotiating the shift to a new master status and living the life of a priest. The priest-abusers saw themselves as able to fulfill the role of priest even as they lived the life of an abuser. (2011, 68)

One respected research project utilized by the John Jay Report was directed by psychologist Eugene Kennedy, which concluded that the experience of sexually deviant behavior among priest-abusers revealed vulnerabilities shared by all human beings, combined with significant deficits in background or formation in the areas of intimacy and empathy.[7] For many Catholic priests, these deficits contributed to psychosocial underdevelopment that was further aggravated by situational stressors, especially among priests in the early phases of their careers. Stressors identified include the transition into parish life, difficult early parish assignments, moves, itinerant ministry, loss of contact with family, lack of feedback, inadequate rewards, overwork, too much responsibility for other people, and time pressures. All of these contributed to loneliness, isolation, and low self-esteem among many priests.[8] Yet strikingly, as the first John Jay Report states, "The most significant conclusion drawn from this data is that no single psychological, developmental, or behavioral characteristic differentiated priests who abused minors from those who did not" (2004, 78).

In its final two chapters, the 2011 report shifts from considering the causes of clerical sexual abuse of minors to focus on the Catholic Church's organizational responses. Although we might be inclined to think that any pathology is about the priests who are abusers, in fact the pathology necessarily includes both the church's response to abuse and the way it establishes and influences the conditions for clergy sexual abuse to occur in the first place. This report had already discussed priestly formation, but two additional aspects bear mentioning. First, the report is quite clear about diocesan leaders' responses being narrowly focused on the treatment of the offending priest and the professional repercussions of their actions. Second, the researchers judge that the church offered a woefully inadequate response to the spiritual and emotional needs of the victims and their families, and when a more robust program of engagement with the victims was finally adopted and encouraged in 1992, many bishops and dioceses were inadequate and laggard in implementing it. Relatedly, the report delineates excuses offered by offenders to diminish their responsibility and justify their lack of empathy for the victims and their families, including sickness, sin, denial of responsibility, denying the victim was really a victim, and raising the possibility that the family was complicit and colluded with the behavior of the abusive priest. Moreover, they justified their actions by invoking God's call to them and the power of forgiveness and reconciliation, but also by deflecting blame onto their superiors for inadequately training them, and by minimizing the seriousness of the harm that they inflicted (2011, 105–12).

In its conclusion, the 2011 John Jay Report recommended three types of prevention policies: educational, situational, and organizational. The final report strongly endorsed the U.S. Bishops' newer approach to ongoing formation of priests, emphasizing the need to address the recurring problems of stress, loneliness, and isolation and to promote leisure and intimacy as a buffer for the stress conditions that can lead to all forms of aberrant behavior. Situational prevention pertains to training programs that foster operational goals: "increase the effort needed to commit acts of abuse...; increase the risks of getting caught...; reduce the rewards...; reduce provocations..., and remove excuses" (120–21). The operational preventions are specified in terms of policies and programs of transparency and accountability.

The John Jay Reports were in part prepared to provide to the U.S. Bishops relevant statistics on the number of clergy accused of sexual abuse of minors. The 2004 report also provided preliminary information about the financial costs to the Catholic Church of clergy sexual abuse of minors (2004, 105–20). It does not, however, include any information about or estimates of the number of people who left the church as a result of these events. Appearing in 2004, 2006, and 2011, these reports did not compile evidence of how the toll of this abuse is manifested in the later lives of victims in terms of alcoholism, drug abuse, depression, post-traumatic stress disorder, self-physical harm, or attempts at suicide. Moreover, the report includes no statistical studies of sexual abuse by former victims of clergy abuse of minors, young people, or adults. While the 2011 report states that the crisis that took place between 1950 and 2010 is a historical crisis of *acts* of sexual abuse, the history of the clerical sexual abuse *crisis* did not subside in 1985, in the 1990s, or in 2000. The history of its receptions and effects in the bodies and psyches of the victims has barely begun to be told, nor has the emotional history of the priests involved. The next two studies introduce these fields of research.

Mary Gail Frawley-O'Dea—Psychoanalytic Analysis of the Abused

Mary Gail Frawley, subsequently Frawley-O'Dea, is a psychoanalyst well known for her work with adult survivors of childhood sexual abuse. In 1994, as Mary Gail Frawley, she coauthored with Jody Messler Davies, also a psychoanalyst, the highly regarded book *Treating the Adult Survivor of Childhood Sexual Abuse: A Psychoanalytic Perspective.*[9] There are many different approaches to the psyche and the human subject that influence how psychoanalysts approach people with past experiences of sexual abuse, which are clearly beyond our focus here. However, some therapists have concentrated in their work on traumatic events in childhood that damage the ability of the person to adapt and develop, while others have sought in therapy to comprehend how traumatic events become combined within current fantasies in the abused person that are self-destructive. Instead of choosing one approach, one theory, one dominant psychological paradigm, Davies and Frawley proposed a "relational treatment model" that provides the therapist a more comprehensive framework when working with a patient.[10] In their words, "our therapeutic model is based...on a constant volleying between regressive reenactment and interpretation of that which is revived through the transference and countertransference constellations that emerge and the progressive unfolding of a new object relationship that takes place between patient and therapist during the course of treatment."[11] As they explain, "it is only through combining psychoanalytic concepts from each major school of [psychoanalytic thought on childhood sexual trauma] emerging from each major school of thought...that we can arrive at an integrated conceptualization of childhood sexual abuse, its sequelae [its secondary results], and its treatment."[12] This more open-ended, multiperspectival approach was well received and utilized.

Eight years after the publication of this coauthored book, Mary Gail Frawly-O'Dea was invited to address the U.S. Bishops Conference on her views of Catholic clergy sexual abuse of minors at their dramatic meeting in Dallas, Texas, in June 2002 after the major revelations of numerous clergy sex abuse cases in Boston, which we will examine in more detail in chapter 4. Five years after this influential address to the U.S. Bishops she published her book *Perversion of Power: Sexual Abuse in the Catholic Church*.[13]

One of Frawley-O'Dea's most important achievements in the theory and practice of psychoanalysis has been to develop an interpersonal and relational approach to the phenomenon of dissociation, the fragmenting or splitting of the sense of self that occurs through traumas such as sex abuse. Such dissociative experiences affect all dimensions of the self: body, mind, memory, senses, and imagination, and the destructive actions that evoke dissociation have become connected with the term *soul murder*. In her own words: "Sexual abuse survivors may be thrown into a regression by something or someone reminiscent of the earlier traumas. No longer firmly located in the present, survivors dissociate—they think, feel, experience their bodies, and behave as the victims they once were, badly confusing themselves and those around them."[14] With the proper support and assistance, Frawley-O'Dea holds out the prospect that these survivors can experience resilience and may come to function well in life, but this is not always the case.

Frawley-O'Dea's training in psychoanalytic practice enabled her to realize that certain kinds of distortion in interpersonal communication and dysfunction in social relationships require the development of critical theories in order to reach a deeper understanding and explanation of the conscious and unconscious factors operative in perpetrators of destructive forms of behavior and in their victims. This discovery enabled her to more effectively name and explore dimensions that contribute to clergy sexual abuse.

In the first part of her book *Perversion of Power*, she explores a set of issues pertaining to how, at certain times and in certain places, suffering has been esteemed and treasured in Christianity, based on a core belief that salvation is achieved by the suffering and death of Jesus Christ, God and man, a doctrine that occupies a central place in Christian belief and practice.[15] Over the church's first few centuries, Frawley-O'Dea argues, these convictions about the value of suffering began to operate as the basis for centralized authority in the church based on Roman views of dominance and submission within a male-controlled form of rule, thereby setting up conditions that were capable of inciting sadomasochistic behavior. This kind of orientation was certainly not the behavior and way of life advanced by Jesus with his companions, whose message was of the coming of the reign, or kingdom, of God. In the scriptural accounts of his life and teaching we find Jesus gathering people together to form an assembly, a community of kinship and fellowship. But over time, the church instead developed ways of exercising power that shaped and controlled the way people understood their relationships with authorities, as well as how they understood their sexual passions and gender differences. Patriarchal political power and the power of the church were eventually intertwined, and along with this development came a new, and also very old, understanding of the identity and roles of women.

Frawley-O'Dea applies her analysis of this pathology of power in the church to offer an explanation of a variety of issues intertwined with the clerical sexual abuse of minors. We can't understand this phenomenon, she argues, without offering an explanation for how people are dealing with their sexual desires and their longings for intimacy, but also how this frequently gets entangled with the repression of sexual passions as a way to live up to the mandated celibate priestly ideal. She relates this, in turn, to the context of growing sexual awakening in the United States in the 1960s. In the later part of the 1960s and throughout the 1970s, more seminarians and priests were acknowledging and struggling with their sexuality, their sexual feelings, and their sexual orientations, and doing so with at least as much excitement, anxiety, and no small amount of bewilderment as their contemporaries in college, graduate school, or in the first years of their careers. As a result, many seminarians and priests left; others sought to remain in priestly ministry but were not always helped or encouraged to be transparent and honest with themselves or their spiritual counselors.

Within this thorny nest of ideas and emotions already introduced, leave it to the psychoanalyst to go even deeper and into, for some, more uncomfortable ideas by exploring how sexual desires— heterosexual, homosexual, bisexual, and in some cases just ambiguous or opaque—can become acted upon in the contexts of the seminary and priestly life. As Frawley-O'Dea clearly acknowledges, there are priests of every sexual orientation who are psychologically integrated and faithfully celibate. But there are others who have engaged in sexual activity with consenting adults, either once or in patterns of sexual relations. There can also be sexually abusive relationships between priests and adult laymen or laywomen, with other priests, or with women religious. To address all these matters in spiritually and psychologically holistic and healthy ways, they need to be discussed in the open by those involved, not only in a therapy session, but for Catholics, also in the context of confession with another priest or with a spiritual counselor, usually a priest.

Too often, however, attempts to do this are stymied or distorted by a culture of secrecy among cardinals, bishops, and clergy and by power dynamics that are employed to threaten outing people for one form of behavior or another, sometimes associated with extortion of favors or money, and with the risk of public scandal. The resulting dysfunction is manifested in many ways, including hypocritical or contradictory behaviors by priests and bishops. As is increasingly understood, for example, men both in the hierarchy and among the clergy who have engaged in egregious sexual acts with boys have been among the most vociferous critics of "homosexuality" and the realities associated with LGBTQ lives. This pattern of secrecy in dealing with the sexual lives of clergy, often combined with the scapegoating of gay priests, is a particularly offensive form of discourse and practice.

Frawley-O'Dea devotes a section of her book to the actions of the Catholic hierarchy and priests as further manifesting the dysfunctions of power within the institutional church. She uses two psychological dynamics not employed in the John Jay Report to offer her assessment. First, she poses the question that has been on the lips and minds of many Catholics: "Where were the pastors?" Across the history of the sexual abuse scandal, far too many bishops were missing in action. They failed to respond to requests to meet with the victims and their families, nor did they take the initiative to reach out to them. The author diagnosed this behavior as "revictimizing the victims" (Frawley-O'Dea, 132). Her second diagnosis pertains to the problem of clericalism, which we will explore later in this chapter. She speaks specifically about the problem of clerical narcissism, that is, a form of behavior in which a person fails to express empathy toward others, including toward the woundedness inflicted by priest-abusers. Like the John Jay Report (2011), she identifies the theology of the ontological change that occurs in priests through the sacrament of ordination as problematic, which contributes to setting priests apart from other humans (Frawley-O'Dea, 166).

In the end, this psychoanalyst holds out the prospect that the revelations of long-held secrets about clergy sexual abuse of minors beginning in the 1980s and through the 1990s, and the scandal's aftermath in the twenty-first century, can shed light on a variety of deeper psychological and sociological pathologies, distortions, and dysfunctions afflicting the church. However, just as the advent of the women's movement in the 1970s brought to light incest and sex abuse against women in different waves over the 1980s and 1990s and now well into this millennium, the tallies of female and male victims of clergy sexual abuse during this period are still being revised. Have we found any ways to bring about more lasting change in the church, or in society at large? These critical theories promote a clearer diagnosis of the pathology, but they also show that the problem is far deeper and wider than previously grasped and that certain issues have as yet been undertheorized. Undertaking the more extensive theoretical work needed to redress this situation may contribute to resilience, better informed resistance, and perhaps even a measure of justice.

Marie Keenan—Assessing the Perpetrators

Irish psychotherapist Marie Keenan is the author of the 2012 book *Child Sexual Abuse and the Catholic Church: Gender, Power, and Organizational Culture*.[16] While Frawley-O'Dea's contribution has been shaped by clinical work especially with adult victims of childhood sexual abuse, Keenan's is especially built upon her work with offending priests. Frawley-O'Dea uses a psychoanalytic approach to the trauma of abuse and the dissociation caused by it that is informed by a diversity of psychoanalytic theories and traditions. By contrast, Keenan indicates that her research and practice draw on "cognitive-behavioral approaches to help the men in therapy for sexual offending find ways of reorienting their lives so that it totally avoids abuse of minors. [This] therapy involved individual, group, and family therapy modalities, as well as accountability meetings, workshops on specific topics, and self-help groups for families" (xix). Members of the offender's social and professional networks, including bishops and religious superiors, would also participate in accountability meetings. Keenan also uses the language of trauma to describe the experiences of sexually abused minors, the wounded quality of that experience, and the recurrent repercussions of abuse, even though, in this work, she never addresses dissociative experiences of victims.

Keenan's cognitive-behavioral approach to therapy is also interwoven with an approach to social science that aims to understand the meanings of human actions, sometimes raising critical theoretical perspectives that are also, like Frawley-O'Dea's approach, open-ended and multiperspectival. She is concerned that in public discourse about clergy sex abuse "the debate is usually limited to typical themes such as deviance, pathology, and betrayal by perpetrators, trauma and damage to victims and their families, and 'cover-up' and betrayal by the Church leaders" (xxii). These categorizations too often restrict inquiry rather than promote deeper understanding and exploration of the possible agency of victims, of their acts of resistance, their resilience, and even the prospects of restorative justice and healing, though in limited ways and not for all those involved. Concerning bishops' responses, Keenan also comments that we need to reflect upon the diverse learning curves of bishops as these have played out during the many phases of this period in history.

Keenan is very insistent, and she restates this claim throughout her work, that her "main aim...is to understand and analyze child sexual abuse by Catholic clergy in its individual and systemic dimensions" (xiv) and to "understand and explain and ultimately prevent in as far as possible, sexual abuse by Catholic clergy" (67). Without minimizing in the least the moral responsibility of individual priests and bishops for their behavior, Keenan is particularly insistent in her 2012 book that the pathology that contributed to clergy sex abuse of minors can be traced back to the Catholic Church's organizational and institutional culture. She associates the responsibility of the church in these matters with the church's moral theology of sexuality, particularly in relation to priesthood and celibacy, as well as with the structures of governance, power relations, and hierarchical authority handed on in seminaries through formation programs (25–34, 234–39). She recognizes that moral theology training in the seminary during the years under investigation in the area of personal ethics tended to be act centered, where men are instructed to "do" or "not do" certain actions. The alternative would be to set actions within a more relational model of responsibility. The lack of this latter framing, Keenan believes, contributed to an emotional deficit and inclined these men toward a perfectionistic approach to their own behavior (82–85).

In this context, Keenan makes the critical point that the most fundamental issue lay not with "rule breakers," but with men in authority over the rule breakers, who were following the institution's rules ("avoid scandal") as they understood them, despite the horror that flowed from this stance. She is particularly interested in the correlation of "loneliness, isolation, and anger" in offending priests (63). When offending clergy are compared to nonoffending clergy, what differentiates the groups is not degrees of loneliness and isolation, but rather, "over-controlled hostility" (62). Equally important, "just as clerical men who sexually abuse minors were not in the main psychological or moral 'deviants' who infiltrated the system," she writes, "neither were the bishops who 'erred' nonconforming deviants who did not obey the institution's rules. On the contrary,...both were rule-keepers in an organization whose very institutional condition gave shape to the contour of the problem" (53). That said, offending priests and bishops who failed to respond to what they should have seen as an obvious disaster in transparent and responsible ways must be held accountable for their actions and inactions.

Keenan shares Frawley-O'Dea's fundamentally feminist orientation to issues of gender and power as these bear upon the presenting issues in clergy sex abuse, but Keenan's method especially emphasizes the power of language or discourse in the formation of the human subject. Her understanding of the way power is influenced by discourse is in important ways drawn from Michel Foucault, the influential French social theorist who has devoted much of his work to analyzing how power operates in social institutions and how language shapes and distorts human identities. Foucault posited that typical, "normative judgments" or opinions do not reflect "'objective' reality." Instead, the judgments that seem obvious to us are drawn from "practices and customs that are reified over time," solidifying through repetition until we believe them to be objectively true. In the process of "reification," the "power relations at play in their creation" are elided. (Think of how racial or gender stereo-types came to be created and understood as "true" over time, in a way that concealed how dominant groups benefit from unques-tioning belief in their validity.) In other words, what counts as "knowledge," or what we think we know, is profoundly influenced by those with the power to insist on the truth of certain state-ments.

What does this have to do with clergy sexual abuse? For Fou-cault, "discourse" (the repetition and absorption of certain phrases and concepts) both shapes and is shaped by power relationships within groups, even when we do not want to see or admit this. The-ology and canon law, among other academic disciplines, contrib-uted to the clergy sex abuse crisis by, for example, promoting the idea of ordination as bringing about an ontological change that made some priests believe and feel that they are apart from and beyond the normal rules of human sexual behavior. They also con-tributed by establishing a sacralized hierarchy that sought to avoid "scandal" above all else, prioritizing the reputation of the church and priests over the needs of victims. In both cases, theological dis-course reinforced and supported a preexisting power arrangement (a hierarchy that set adults above children, priests above laity, and, in the end, the reputation of the church above the truth) while pre-tending that it was simply reflecting and defending timeless truths. This is how "discourse" becomes, in Foucault's words, "a means of control and a method of domination" (cited in Keenan, 97).

Based on her concerns about the power of discourse and the way in which discourse invisibly supports power, Keenan explores in the final part of her book how sexuality and gender are under-stood, especially in the Catholic Church and by priests in particu-lar (part 3, 129–257). In her judgment, "celibacy is not the problem that gives rise to sexual abuse of minors," but mandatory clerical celibacy is a topic that should be discussed openly in the church. The real issue with sexuality and gender is that Catholic sexual ethics and the theology of priesthood "'problematize' the body and erotic sexual desire and emphasize chastity and purity over a relational ethic for living....This theology of sexuality contributes to self-hatred, shame, and personal failure, and needs serious theological examination and revision" (235). Celibacy, then, isn't the cause of clergy sexual abuse of minors, but the approach to gender and sexuality that undergirds it is a crucial contributing factor.

Keenan asserts that offending and nonoffending clergy alike often have a questionable and, in some cases, contestable understanding of masculinity. One might ask how widely this theory might apply in diverse global cultures, but it seems plausible as a hypothesis to explore in various settings. To describe it, she uses the term *hegemonic masculinity*, a category formulated about twenty-five years ago by sociologists to characterize a particular domineering way in which men often behave, and which is assumed to be the only acceptable type of masculinity. She proposes that among Catholic priests there are several prevailing versions of masculinity. The most important and often considered ideal variety is the hegemonic type, which incorporates an exacting approach to "masculine" perfection, celibacy, and chastity. This priest is a rule follower. If he doesn't follow the rules and live up to the ideal by falling short of perfection, he humanly fails, he religiously sins, and he has revealed, at least to himself, his weakness: weakness that, for this version of clerical masculinity, is a source of shame and self-recrimination.

These priests have been trained to be apprehensive about sexual desire, about emotional intimacy with women and men, and even about genuine friendship with other priests. They are "seen as set apart and set above" (245), which provides the source of their institutional power in the church and in society. They are inclined to repress anger and avoid conflict, and they have a low tolerance for tension, paradox, and ambiguity in life. These men are not inclined to share power and promote teamwork and collegiality. Keenan describes this particular version of masculinity as Perfect Celibate Clerical Masculinity. The group that embraces this ideal typically includes offending clergy, but others also express these traits. These priests can be officious and remote with adult women and men. With young people and children that are abused they can also act in condescending ways, but they can also see these children as a channel for reclaiming the friendship, intimacy, and, frankly, human contact that has eluded them in their adult life.

Keenan mentions three other versions of clerical masculinity, each with many comparable traits and details. Priests expressing Compassionate Celibate Clerical Masculinity are aware of their emotional and sexual motivations. Some may act on this awareness with another adult, female or male, and have an intense emotional relationship. Certain priests may even have sexual encounters, episodic occasions accompanied by a real sense of guilt, yet not shame, which they seek to move beyond, often in discussion with a spiritual director.

By contrast, men expressing Incongruous Celibate Clerical Masculinity (the term *incongruous* means "inappropriate" or "unsuitable") have sexual encounters, either with women or men depending on their sexual orientation, but experience no guilt despite their formal commitment to celibacy. Some of these men engage in a double life with a long-term relationship with an adult woman or man.

Keenan identifies a fourth style of masculinity that she names without further description as "a version that is built on very deep faith and holiness" (244). This formulation is enigmatic, and maybe it is intended to be. Without further clarification, this depiction runs the risk of avoiding scrutinizing questionable sexual behavior and relationships in order to hold priests accountable.

Keenan concludes by strongly reiterating her conviction about the systemic character of the pathology: "Sexual abuse is inevitable given the meaning system that is taught by the Catholic Church and to which many priests adhere. The contradictions force failure and increase shame and a way of living that encourages sexually deviant behavior" (255).

Theological Diagnoses

We have thus far examined three approaches to evaluating clerical sexual abuse of minors. All three have identified multiple causes based, respectively, on (1) the historical, cultural, and empirical data and analysis in the John Jay Reports, (2) the multiperspectival relational model used in the psychoanalytic approach of Mary Gail Frawley-O'Dea, and (3) Marie Keenan's treatment shaped by a cognitive-behavioral approach to psychotherapy, a critical social theory analysis of gender and power, and an approach to social structures based on organizational culture studies. Now our attention shifts to how the Catholic Church theologically assesses clergy sexual abuse of minors and episcopal concealment of this behavior, based on the doctrine of sin and specifically an approach to personal, social, and structural sin as this has developed in recent papal teachings by John Paul II, Benedict XVI, and Francis. The views of these three popes reveal how classic sources and stances in Catholic theology have informed a dynamic and debated tradition.

In general, these three popes' statements on sin agree with the John Jay research team, Frawley-O'Dea, and Keenan on one central conviction: that clergy who sexually abuse children must be held personally accountable for their actions. However, the social scientists maintain that the abusive sexual behaviors attributed to the intentional choices of individuals also have multiple contributing social and cultural influences. By contrast, the long-standing tradition of Catholic theology has consistently traced the humanly perpetrated harm and destruction of individual lives and communities back to personal sin.

However, this basic line of argument about how classic theological sources evaluated harmful sexual behavior has always been more complicated, insofar as these sources were influenced by the philosophical theories of the Stoics, Plato, and Aristotle, among others, and the analysis of the "eight evil thoughts" developed by Evagrius of Pontus and the "eight vices" by John Cassian, which in turn were reflected upon in the teachings on the seven deadly sins, and corresponding treatment of the healing power of grace and the virtues in the theologies of Augustine and Thomas Aquinas. The people who handed on these traditions of Christian spirituality, pastoral practice, and theology tended to speak of sin using two sets of analogies or metaphors: sin could be thought of as a crime requiring judgment and penalty, or as a disease requiring a cure. These two models, legal and medical, have persisted over time as

Christians continued to meditate on the causes of sin and on God's responses to its reality.

While early theologians such as Evagrius of Pontus and Augustine spoke of personal sin as framed within and influenced by the mores of the social groups that we inherit and inhabit, Catholic moral theology as it later developed around the sacrament of confession focused on a person's free choice to commit a specific physical or mental act. This basic way of thinking became increasingly complicated in the modern period based on deeper reflection on various forms of conflict and contestation: the long history of anti-Semitism that led to the mass killings of Jews in Nazi Germany; the influence of colonialism and its ongoing impact on racism, nationalism, immigration, and refugees; and the adverse effects of capitalism. To what extent are our personal decisions and acts shaped by these social systems, even as our personal decisions and acts contribute to their maintenance? As we have seen in the previous section, Michel Foucault's thinking about how "discourse" and "power" shape each other also raises a set of questions about the relationship between personal sin and what we might call "social," "structural," and "systemic" sin.

The bishops at the Second Vatican Council reaffirmed the church's enduring convictions about the source of so much human grief being personal sin. Yet the council also acknowledged that impacts of personal sin adversely affected social circumstances, the social order, and the social sphere.[17] After the council, as increasing attention was given to destructive patterns of social injustice in various communities, the question arose, notably among theologians and bishops in Latin America, whether any social entity can be identified as sinful. The categories of sinful situations, and subsequently social sin and structures of sin, were used in documents prepared by the Latin American Bishops Conference during their meetings in Medellín in 1968, in Puebla in 1979, in Santo Domingo in 1992, and at Aparecida in 2007.[18] These views received increasing attention from bishops and theologians around the world. And this expanding understanding of sin also had a profound impact on how bishops and theologians analyzed clergy sex abuse and episcopal complicity.

A Thomist Orientation—John Paul II

In 1983, representative bishops from around the world were convened by Pope John Paul II to participate in an assembly called a synod of bishops in order to reflect upon issues related to reconciliation and penance in the church and world, a topic chosen by the pope as meriting attention. At their meeting, the bishops discussed issues pertaining to manifestations of social and structural sin; and in 1984, John Paul II issued a post-synodal document, *Reconciliation and Penance*, offering his own interpretation of the synod's findings. In this document, John Paul II became the first pope to introduce and authorize the use of a distinction between personal and social sin, thereby also acknowledging the category of social sin used by many bishops at the 1983 synod.[19] John Paul II described social sin in terms of the social effects of individual personal sins and proposed that social sin refers to the ways in which personal sin and injustice become embodied within social structures. Social sins are thus "the result of the accumulation and concentration of many personal sins," and are "rooted in personal sin, and thus always linked to the concrete acts of individuals."[20]

In his 1987 encyclical *On Social Concern*, John Paul II further developed his teaching on social sin by delineating its various meanings. First, social sin can be associated with personal sins that adversely affect and harm other individuals and communities. Second, some sins can be understood as social sin because they are committed directly against other members of society and thus are a violation of various social goods: love of neighbor, justice, freedom, the dignity of another, and the common good. And third, social sin also pertains, by analogy, to sinful patterns of relationships among communities, groups, and peoples.[21] John Paul II thus insists that when the church speaks of social sin in this third way, the term is being used only analogically: that is, the term *sin* is properly attributed only to personal sins and cannot be applied in a literal sense to social groups, structures, or institutions. As a result, we cannot, strictly speaking, blame groups, social systems, structures, or institutions when there is a problem. We should instead seek the conversion of individual persons who impact social structures. It is not difficult to see how this might be applied to evaluations of the clergy sexual abuse scandal.

John Paul II subsequently applied this distinction in his analyses of economics and pro-life issues,[22] and in his 1995 encyclical, *That All May Be One*, he acknowledged social sinfulness in ecumenical relations between the Catholic Church and other Christian churches, as we see here:

> Christian unity is possible, provided that we are humbly conscious of having sinned against unity and are convinced of our need for conversion. Not only personal sins must be forgiven and left behind, but also social sins, which is to say the sinful "structures" themselves which have contributed and can still contribute to division and to the reinforcing of division.[23]

In the decade leading up to the turn of the new millennium John Paul II devoted considerable attention to the church's need to repent of its sinfulness.[24] This culminated in an official Day of Pardon, during which a prayer service was held in St. Peter's Basilica in the Vatican to recall and to offer repentance for the sins of the church. John Paul II applied the teaching on social sin to the history of the church in unprecedented and at times in moving ways, and yet he affirmed the purity and holiness of the church itself as an institution. It is the sons and daughters of the church who sin; one cannot speak of the sinfulness of the church, even in cases such as anti-Semitism, a sin in which a vast majority of all Christians in history participated.[25]

An important limitation of John Paul II's position is that he did not articulate how social sin operates at the unconscious and unintentional levels in both society and the church. As theologian Gregory Baum concludes, John Paul II came to recognize structures of sin as institutional realities, but he was unable to recognize "the unconscious, nonvoluntary dimension of social sin—to the blindness produced in persons by the dominant culture, blindness that prevents them from recognizing the evil dimensions of their social reality."[26] In his emphasis on the intentional character of personal sin, he failed to draw out the implications of his teachings on social sin in terms of how it operates through structures of power in cultures, organizational policies, and civil law.

He could not, therefore, articulate the implications of "social sin" either for understanding society's grievous failings, or for the promotion of fundamental social change. Margaret Pfeil makes the point clearly: "John Paul II is cognizant of the blinding effect of ideology and the almost automatic operation of economic and political institutions, but his awareness of this unconscious aspect of sin stands in tension with his strong emphasis on personal responsibility."[27] He was therefore unable to clarify the relationship between personal responsibility for sin and "the unconscious, indeliberate activity involved in the creation and maintenance of sinful systems, institutions, and structures."[28]

John Paul II's teaching on sin reflects his deep commitments to an understanding of the human person and to a natural law approach to sexual ethics as developed by Thomas Aquinas, which espouses an act-centered approach to moral decision-making and sin, based on and evaluated according to human intentions. His Thomistic orientation was consistent with his philosophical commitment to phenomenology, which is likewise dedicated to the central role of individual human intentions and intentional analysis. As a result, while Pope John Paul II is highly regarded for his leadership in many areas of Catholic social teaching, he is criticized for, in the words of Marie Keenan, "his failure to take decisive action in relation to child sexual abuse by Catholic clergy for which he is often criticized. His handling of the two cases...involv[ing] Vienna's Cardinal Hans Hermann Groër and Marcial Maciel Degollado, founder of the Legionaries of Christ," is especially telling.[29] John Paul's insistence on the personal character of sin in the church appears to have contributed to his inability to face the cultural and systemic dimensions of clergy abuse and episcopal malfeasance.

An Augustinian Assessment—Benedict XVI

Benedict XVI, John Paul II's successor, is acknowledged for his deep learning in theology and in particular his commitment to the theology of Augustine of Hippo. Augustine is renowned for his many writings across the spectrum of theological topics, and of particular relevance here for his elaboration of the doctrine of original sin and its relationship to personal sin. Pope Benedict XVI never used John Paul II's categories of social sin and structures of sin in his papal writings. This absence is especially notable in *Caritas in Veritate*, his 2009 social encyclical, even though in his treatment of economic issues he clearly acknowledges the need to advance social change at the structural level.[30] This omission is consistent with Benedict's long-standing critique of any attempt in Catholic theology to use Marxist categories such as class struggle to analyze the causes of social injustice and poverty. Thus, in *Caritas in Veritate*, Benedict instead speaks of "the presence of original sin in social conditions and in the structures of society," but makes no reference to social sin, to the involvement of groups or institutions in systemic injustice, or to the formation and maintenance of structures of sins.[31]

The impact of Benedict's views on personal sin are especially evident in his approach to clerical sexual abuse of minors. Beginning in 2001, as head of the Congregation for the Doctrine of the Faith, Joseph Ratzinger (the future Pope Benedict) became responsible as a matter of canon law for reaching judgments in certain cases of accusations against priests, including accusations of sexual abuse of minors. It was his responsibility to decide whether priest offenders who had abused minors should be removed from the priesthood ("laicization"), a canonical procedure, based on his analysis of the ecclesiological repercussions of a personal sin. Subsequently, during his papacy, Benedict spoke of clerical sexual abuse as "so much filth," but he continued to address it as a problem of personal sin, to be addressed as such, and not in terms of social or structural or institutional sin, nor in terms of criminal activity.

Pope Benedict urged that the church's teachings against such abusive behavior by priests must be clarified and better taught, and that justice should be administered more swiftly, all the while caring for the victims and their healing. His position, however, was incapable of illumining the collective roles of secrecy about and cover-up of the acts of abusive priests. Nor could his position shed light on the complicity and hypocrisy of local, national, or international priests, bishops, and cardinals of the church involved in clerical sex abuse. Personal sin is addressed, but systemic issues are not thoroughly pursued despite his occasional hint, as in his 2010 letter on clergy sex abuse to the people of Ireland, that systemic factors including "inadequate procedures," "insufficient... formation," "a tendency in society to favor...authority figures," and "a misplaced concern for the reputation of the Church" might have been involved.[32]

An Ignatian Discernment—Francis

To conclude this chapter let us consider Pope Francis's views on personal and social sin and its implications for his approach to the clergy sex abuse scandal. In thinking about all three popes, it helps to keep in mind the major formative influences on each of them. John Paul II's positions on human intentionality in an act-centered approach to moral theology were deeply shaped by his understanding of the philosophy and theology of Thomas Aquinas and modern phenomenology, which is influenced by the views of Aquinas, as providing the framework to think about personal sin and its derivative impact on social relationships, communities, societies, structures, and global realities. Benedict XVI's stance, by contrast, is marked by his lifelong dedication to the theology of Augustine of Hippo, and thus emphasizes the importance of original sin and its impact on personal sin and on social situations, both of which reveal the disordered loves of sinful persons.

Pope Francis, by contrast, has been profoundly influenced by the spiritual practices of Ignatius of Loyola, notably his *Spiritual Exercises*, which emphasize the role of the examination of conscience in the personal endeavor of spiritual discernment. This examination concentrates on an individual's sins amid their entire history of sinfulness.

Over the course of his ministerial life, Francis has stated in different ways that personal sin can lead to corruption in relationships and institutions, which can result in abuses of power. Like

John Paul II, Francis denounces the social ramifications of sin in society as the embodiment of personal sins, but unlike John Paul, and interestingly given his Latin American background, Francis very rarely uses the terms *social sin* and *structures of sin*. Often, he speaks of personal sin as the result of an undisciplined heart: when we do not master our passions, we harm the self and others.

In 1990, however, he explored more explicitly a connection between "sin and corruption."[33] Personal sin can result in corporate corruption in society and in the church. Fifteen years later, in a preached retreat with bishops, he said that those who have succumbed to their passions "can sow discord and division, resort to betrayal in order to gain followers, [and] *establish unjust social structures* in the heart of a community or diocese through pharisaical attitudes."[34] This kind of reasoning undergirds his acknowledgment of the role of structural sin in the financial crisis in Argentina in 2001–2, when he detects the impact of sinful individuals on structural corruption and reaches the judgment that "this economy kills."[35]

Before Francis began exploring the connection between clericalism and clergy sexual abuse of minors, he perceived in clericalism a crucial example of personal sin leading to ecclesial corruption. In a 2011 interview, then Cardinal Bergoglio described clericalism as a contagious disease that is passed from clergy to laypeople. As he puts it, "We priests tend to clericalize the laity. We do not realize it, but it is as if we infect them with our own disease. And the laity—not all, but many—ask us on their knees to clericalize them, because it is more comfortable to be an altar server than the protagonist of a lay path."[36]

Clericalist priests and bishops "infantilize" the laity, yet laity too often wish for the priest to exercise all the leadership so that they don't need to be active leaders in the life and ministry of the church. In a special mark of his pontificate, Francis often challenges everyone "to overcome clericalism and to increase lay responsibility."[37] He goes on to argue that excessive clericalism works in tandem with spiritual worldliness, manifested in various forms of ecclesiastical narcissism that focus priests and bishops on internal church matters rather than on reaching out to the poor, the marginalized, and those in need of healing and justice.[38]

Pope Francis's critique of clericalism is one of the many distinguishing features of his papacy, but it is matched in its significance, and perhaps even surpassed, by his Christmas season addresses to the Roman curia over a number of years after he became pope, in which he summoned curial officials to examine their consciences and to be open to conversion and the reform of the curia in personal behavior, cultural patterns, and systemic reform. In the first address, which took place on December 22, 2014, Francis led the Roman curia in an examination of conscience describing fifteen kinds of sin associated with their positions of authority.[39] Building on the image of the church as the Body of Christ and using the ancient medical model of sin, Francis observes that the curia, "like any human body,...is also exposed to diseases, malfunctioning, infirmity." He goes on to identify some of the "more common 'curial diseases'" that threaten the curia's vitality and the effectiveness of their service.[40]

Many of these fifteen "diseases" can be associated with the particular ambitions, temperaments, and pastoral life experiences of those in the curia, a group of very powerful men with unknown forms of accountability. But the first and the last diseases identified reflect more collective problems. The first is the "disease of thinking we are 'immortal,' 'immune' or downright 'indispensable,' neglecting the need for regular check-ups." This reality manifests as a "pathology of power,...from a superiority complex, from a narcissism which passionately gazes at its own image and does not see the image of God on the face of others, especially the weakest and those most in need." This formulation could be considered a particular species of clericalism and spiritual worldliness, a kind of pathology associated with the exercise of power and authority, a posited superiority or sovereignty in relation to those outside the center, such as those in a local church, a national church, and in the global church. Curial centralization is the specific form of clericalism here identified.

The fifteenth sin is "the disease of worldly profit, of forms of self-exhibition, [which] turns his service into power, and his power into a commodity in order to gain worldly profit or even greater power." Thus, Francis begins and ends his meditation with power and greed.[41] This particular formula resembles John Paul II's expression in *On Social Concern*: "Among the actions and attitudes opposed to the will of God, the good of neighbor and the 'structures' created by them, two are very typical: on the one hand, the all-consuming desire for profit, and on the other, the thirst for power, with the intention of imposing one's will upon others."[42] However, there is good reason to wonder whether Francis's treatment exceeds that by John Paul II. Francis's remarks on power and greed may make a special claim, since they are associated not only with clergy in administrative roles but with men who are central figures in a hierarchical structure that is global in reach. A global matrix of power and greed reverberates throughout the universal church.

Let me end this consideration of Pope Francis's analysis of sin by examining two of his statements about the systemic sin of clericalism and episcopal concealment, which were influenced by two different events that took place in 2018. When Pope Francis visited the north of Chile in January 2018, a reporter asked him whether he supported the controversial appointment of a bishop who was associated with a priest accused of sexual abuse. In response Francis said, "The day they bring me proof against the bishop, then I will speak. There is not a single proof against him. This [is] calumny [slander]! Is that clear?" His comment elicited a public protest. In response to the escalating controversy, Francis asked two Vatican officials to arrange meetings in appropriate countries to interview people involved. After they completed their investigation at the end of February, he sent a letter on April 8 to the bishops involved summoning them to meet with him, and on May 31, 2018, sent a letter apologizing both to the abused individuals and to the entire people of Chile.

Francis was personally implicated in this public controversy in Chile, which called for his own process of repentance and conversion pertaining not only to clerical abuse but also to episcopal concealment. Subsequently, in the aftermath of the release of the Pennsylvania Grand Jury Report on August 14, 2018, Francis issued in response "A Letter to the People of God" on August 20, 2018.

In this letter he acknowledged "the suffering endured by many minors due to sexual abuse, the abuse of power, and the abuse of conscience." "Clericalism," he wrote, "whether fostered by priests themselves or by lay persons, leads to an excision in the ecclesial body that supports and helps to perpetuate many of the evils that we are condemning today. To say 'no' to abuse to is say an emphatic 'no' to all forms of clericalism." With this formulation, Francis does not say that clericalism causes sex abuse, but indirectly, perhaps even opaquely, he implies it.

No modern pope has devoted so much attention to diagnosing pathologies and corruption in the church associated with clericalism, ecclesiastical centralization, and curial and papal sovereignty. Francis may not use the terms *social sin* and *structures of sin*, but he has identified the social effects of personal sin and the embodiment of personal sins in ecclesial structures and systems. This combination of pathologies of power and greed is operative in organized criminal behavior in society, but it can also be detected in curial temptations and actions, and it resonates strongly with the behaviors exhibited by cardinals and bishops in the scandal of clerical sexual abuse of minors.

As we have observed, the position of Pope Francis on sin appears comparable to that of John Paul II. Yet in his official addresses and writings to date, Francis neither introduces nor employs explicitly a distinction between personal sin and social sin. Instead, he has, in the spirit of Ignatius, explored the implications of sin in and for individuals, and he has acknowledged and taught that a sinful self can lead to a corrupted structure and system. Different levels of disease and pathology can be operative not only in the behavior of corporations (social bodies), structures, and systems, but also in the cultures that sustain them in a way that become operational in unintentional and unconscious ways of being reproduced over generations.

These are examples of corruption and the abuse of power in social bodies, institutions, structures, and systems that have been spoken about by Pope Francis. In his treatment of clericalism, we see an especially clear instance of a disease and pathology that is operative not only among individual priests, but also in groups, dioceses, religious orders, episcopal conferences, and in the Roman curia.

Conclusion

Let me close this chapter by inviting readers to consider and to discuss the following: How do these interdisciplinary interlocutors—sociologists who investigate patterns of criminal behavior and contributing organizational cultures, psychoanalysts who have studied the victims of sexual crimes and their abusers, and the last three popes who have analyzed personal, social, structural, and systemic sin—compare in their assessments of the causes of clergy sex abuse of minors and its episcopal concealment? Are there issues that have not yet been thoroughly explored? And how could our efforts to interrogate, understand, and explain other manifestations of complex sins, such as racism, shed light on clergy sexual abuse of minors and episcopal concealment?

Chapter 3

Prophetic Voices, Protests, and Movements

How do the victims of clerical sexual abuse engage in public protests in which they can voice their laments before clergy and bishops? And how do their allies, witnesses, and advocates respond to the laments of those who have been violated as they search for justice?

The church controversy we have been investigating here would not be widely known either in or outside the church were it not for these groups of people courageously speaking out. The practices of secrecy and cover-up by those in authority aimed to sweep many horrible injustices under the rug to avoid scandal and to guard against any undermining of the hierarchical and clerical authority of the church or its wealth. Only the protests of the violated and of their allies led to the recent efforts to bring this scandal to light.

Many victims who have come to identify themselves as survivors become actively engaged, at least for a period of their lives, in public forms of resistance and protest against the priests and bishops who abused and maltreated them. Allies who paid attention to the laments of survivors and listened to their grievances, animated by their outrage, have also joined in developing public ways to respond. In some instances, as we will see, these public responses were based on previously utilized methods. Besides being decisive manifestations of crisis, conflict, and controversy in the church since the Reformation, such responses cumulatively make up the most dramatic instances of reform movements in the modern church. They also illuminate important avenues for confronting other kinds of controversies that contemporary Catholics have encountered in their communities of faith.

Here we focus on the interval since 1950. How have people who witnessed this horrible series of crimes responded? This chapter introduces a range of examples of protests and of calls for accountability. We will examine four prominent types of public strategies as these have been pursued by four types of individuals and groups:

1. *Victim-survivors* who, in response to the crimes themselves, but much more often because of the deficient and often harmful responses given by bishops and their representatives, go beyond their own efforts at pursuing self-care and healing to develop tactics of resistance and public protest and propose strategies of reform.

2. *Allies of victim-survivors* include parents, siblings, family members, friends, and many people who have no formal connection with survivors but feel profoundly enraged and a deep solidarity with survivors and wish, with them, to voice their anger and insist on fundamental structural reform in the church and justice for those violated.

3. *Witnesses* in the media who investigate and report the secrets and lies surrounding clergy sexual abuse.

4. *Advocates and sometimes arbiters of justice*, a category that represents agents of, and courses of action taken by, the legal justice system that bring individuals and the church to public accountability for clergy sex abuse.

I will identify the stances taken by these four groups of people as instances of *prophetic action*, even though the people involved might not use this terminology to describe their actions and their motivation. Nevertheless, as we will see, they provide inspiring and important examples of prophetic actions today.

Speaking Out: Prophetic *Parrhesia*

Why speak about protests and movements that have arisen in response to clerical sexual abuse as prophetic? Prophets are often described as people that have identified with those who have suffered some injustice or are the victims of such injustice themselves. They have felt compelled to take a stand against the perpetrators or institutions that have caused or been complicit in such acts of injustice and violation. Scholars of the Hebrew Scriptures, the Christian Scriptures, or Islamic scriptures and traditions customarily recognize prophets as individuals who are caught up in a dramatic encounter with God that is sometimes described in terms of intimacy and friendship, while at other times in terms of fear and trembling before God the source and goal of all that is. This relationship between God and the prophet entails being drawn into a passionate engagement with those who are especially beloved by God—the victimized, the marginalized, and the oppressed. The prophet's love of God combines with a passionate preference for those suffering injustices and becomes combustible into a righteous rage toward perpetrators and institutional structures that cause such injustice.

This divine fire of love and outrage toward the unrighteous is given expression in prophetic witness—to use the Greek word *parrhesia* (παρρησία), bold honest speech in which the consequences of speaking out and acting up can be at risk. This is the prophetic impetus for what has been called in the modern period "speaking truth to power," whether civic or business leaders or ordained clerical officials. Prophetic witness is not only associated with prophetic critique through tactical public protests and denunciations, but also with the conjuring of the productive prophetic imagination in which the laments of the victim-survivors and prophetic critique provide the impetus for strategic endeavors to imagine new social configurations of systems, social structures, and cultures that provide healing and a new hopeful future. Prophetic witnesses are not only identified as Jews, Christians, and Muslims who draw on the inspiration of their own religious traditions when they offer prophetic critiques and exercise their prophetic imaginations. There are many religious seekers as well as people who are decidedly not religious, but who are associated with protests and constructive strategic actions in response to injustices, that would be and are called prophetic because they witness in word and deed on behalf of justice in solidarity with those who have been violated.

This chapter examines how victims of clergy sex abuse by priests and bishops are leading examples today of prophetic convictions and actions, whether they remain religious or not. We will also learn about many groups who have joined in solidarity with these victims and together represent a prophetic movement in formation, bringing together religious and nonreligious agents. Specifically, we will examine people in diverse kinds of public media who, regardless of their religious affiliation (or lack thereof), fulfill a distinctive prophetic function in civil society by investigating and reporting on injustices, crimes, and cover-ups. Finally, we will examine the role of grand juries in taking on a prophetic function in civil society.

These prophetic figures have collectively shed a bright light on the dysfunctional behavior associated with the Catholic Church and on the wounded people that behavior has left in its wake. They have been crucial catalysts in awakening people to the fact that these crimes are not simply about "a few bad apples" besmirching the purity of the church. Rather, they have brought to the attention of various audiences in church and society the deeper patterns of behavior associated with the wickedness of organized corruption, complicity, and the maintenance of harmful cultures. These prophetic groups have challenged people to recognize in the horrors of clergy sex abuse not simply the result of personal sin, nor only the consequences of original sin, but the infestation of sin in cultures and in structures, operating in far-reaching networks of power and greed that are rightly associated with clericalism, patriarchy, and misogyny.

Pope Francis has often encouraged people in both church and society to exercise courageous and honest speech in practicing missionary discipleship, but also when speaking up against acts of injustice and false witness. He uses the Greek term *parrhesia* that the Apostle Paul and other early church writers employed to support the need for boldness in speaking in the church and in civil society.[1] This activity of *parrhesia*—honest, courageous, and potentially dangerous speech—is also closely associated with prophetic discourse.[2]

Regularly, victims, allies, witnesses, and advocates who engage in courageous, honest prophetic speech and action have been publicly repudiated by certain cardinals, bishops, clergy, and lay faithful who accuse them of seeking to undermine and even destroy the church. These vitriolic and sometimes personal accusations are in keeping with the entire history of prophetic speech and action directed at the powerful; often, they reveal a deafness and hypocrisy among church leaders who level such accusations against the truth that is being spoken to them. All of these dynamics are discernable in the four different trajectories of prophetic critique, denunciation, and calls for accountability and reparation we will now examine.

Victim-Survivors: Networks of the Abused

There are various reasons why those who suffered sexual abuse by priests organized into groups to express their grievances against priest perpetrators and their bishops and representatives who had failed to meet with them or discredited their stories of abuse. The data between 1950 and 2017 treated in chapter 1 reported that the number of incidents of abuse rose steadily during the 1960s and 1970s, reaching high points in the late 1960s through the late 1970s before beginning a steady decline throughout the remainder of the century. Of the approximately fifty incidents of clerical sexual abuse of minors now assumed or known to have taken place during the 1950s (2004, 34), only 5 percent were reported around the time they occurred. As the 2011 John Jay study states,

> Although the majority of abuse incidents had occurred by 1985, most incidents had not yet been reported to the dioceses. If only the 10,667 incidents of abuse reported in the *Nature and Scope* study are considered, 80.5 percent, or four out of five incidents of abuse, had taken place by 1985, but only 810 incidents had been reported to dioceses by that time. This discrepancy is the result of a significant delay in the reporting of most incidents. (2011, 9)

Many victims resisted reporting what happened to them until long after the abuse occurred. This can be attributed to the kinds of psychological wounds the abuse had inflicted, but also to apprehensions about the challenges of taking a public stance. Yet ten, twenty, and thirty years later, as numerous victims reported to dioceses that they had been violated, many of these people also joined groups of survivors for spiritual and psychological support. Some people chose to participate in groups that organized public protests, directed at bishops or other church officials, and in these initiatives, survivors were often joined by family members and friends.

Historian Brian Clites has researched the formation in Chicago of two national survivor organizations that by 1991 had gathered more than three hundred members.[3] He tells the story of Jeanne Miller and Marilyn Steffel, who founded a group called Victims of Clergy Abuse, or LINKUP, which operated from 1982 until 2005. In 1988 with the support and guidance of Miller and Steffel, Barbara Blaine started the Survivors Network of Those Abused by Priests, SNAP, which is still operative today.

Barbara Blaine merits special consideration. She was sexually abused by a priest between 1969 and 1974, beginning when she was thirteen years old after seventh grade. She was psychologically and spiritually wounded, and her memories of being abused were repressed for over ten years, until 1985, when reporter Jason Berry published an article in the widely read *National Catholic Reporter* on the notorious case of Gilbert Gauthe, the priest from Lafayette, Louisiana, who admitted to abusing thirty-seven children.[4] Reading the article initiated Blaine's recovery of memory fragments from her abuse. She returned to her home to tell her parents what had transpired, and in 1986 she confronted the priest who had abused her. His religious order and archdiocese failed to address the situation by removing this priest from active ministry until 1989, even though he remained a threat to the communities that he served. After a long struggle, Blaine, who was not only abused by this priest but was also violated by the mistreatment she received from church authorities, was awarded a financial settlement from the religious order and the archdiocese responsible for the priest who abused her.

During this time Blaine became close to Jeanne Miller, who was the mother of a son abused by a priest. Also, immensely significant was the support and advice she received from Patty Crowley, who had a long history of church and social activism in the Chicago area, leading the Christian Family Movement during the 1950s and '60s, with her husband, Pat.[5] Miller and Crowley, and the example of Dorothy Day and the Catholic Workers, inspired and encouraged Blaine's efforts to form victims' support groups that aimed to address the misuse of clerical and episcopal power in areas that affected children and women.

Blaine was trained as a lawyer and also earned a master of divinity degree in theology. She had experience as a social activist with Pax Christi, a Catholic antiwar group, and subsequently had dedicated herself to years of intense involvement in the Catholic Worker movement, inspired by its founder, Dorothy Day, who combined a deep spirituality with activism on labor issues, poverty, and pacifism. Following Day's model, Blaine negotiated the use of a home owned by the Archdiocese of Chicago to serve as a "House of Hospitality," providing a place for needy women and food services for the poor. Her wide-ranging experience as a spiritually motivated social activist contributed to her organizing work on behalf of those abused by priests.

Blaine's sexual abuse was the source of her righteous anger, which motivated her prophetic critique of what she called the clerical and hierarchical narcissism that fed into a network of abusive ecclesial power. Her abuse by a priest and her difficult struggles with the bishop and religious superior who were responsible for the priest who abused her in active ministry, combined with her spirituality, Catholic activism, legal background, and involvement with the marginalized in society, provided a profound combination of factors that led to her launching the Survivors Network of Those Abused by Priests (SNAP). She envisioned this organization as comprising a network of abused people whose experiences had made them painfully aware of the need to resist and protest against a corrupt system of power in the institutional Catholic Church.

SNAP earned a reputation for being the earliest, largest, and most effective advocacy group of victims of clergy sexual abuse. From its beginning, SNAP members insisted on being identified as survivors, people who would not succumb to victimization but would engage in activism. At first in the Chicago area, and later in chapters across the United States, the group reached out to those sexually abused as children by priests. They developed forms of support that included human contact and community among abuse survivors and access to professionals who could offer psychological and legal assistance as survivors sought healing and recompense for the many forms of damage that had been done. SNAP was particularly vigilant in working to assure that priest offenders were not preying on other children and to hold bishops accountable who had repeatedly transferred priest-abusers to different parishes, cities, states, and countries, all the while cultivating tactics of silence, cover-up, avoidance, and generally failing to listen, support, or respond with the kinds of pastoral care or reparative action needed.

SNAP started in 1988 when Blaine recruited about two dozen victims to support one another by means of phone calls and mail. They gathered in Chicago for their first national meeting in 1991 and in San Francisco in 1992. At the 1992 meeting Blaine met David Clohessy, also a survivor, who became a longtime friend and collaborator in the further development of SNAP as a national organization. When the *Boston Globe* Spotlight stories began breaking in 2002, the numbers of victims contacting SNAP grew precipitously, and a new office was set up to respond to the burgeoning interest.[6] As Clites records,

> In 2001, SNAP had less than five hundred paying members; by the end of 2002 it claimed 2,000 members; by the end of fiscal year 2003, SNAP reported 6,000 supporters; and today [2015] it boasts more than 10,000 dues-paying members. These membership statistics provide additional evidence that it was Boston 2002 that made possible Blaine's formidable empire of victims, attorneys, and secular donors. Regional offices began to appear in the U.S. and then in cities in countries around the world.[7]

As of December 2018 there were over twenty-five thousand survivors from around the world on SNAP's membership rolls.

What is particularly prophetic about SNAP? Their members, whether survivors or allies, are recognized for their faithful prophetic witness through protests against clergy perpetrators of sexual abuse of children and the vulnerable, and their regular, public protests against bishops for their complicity in these crimes and cover-ups at the semiannual assemblies of the United States Catholic Conference of Bishops, and also at major award ceremonies and fundraising events for Catholic cardinals. SNAP's actions symbolize prophetic judgments and denunciations against the clerical desecration of the dignity of human beings who are made in the image of God and abusers' violent acts of injustice against their human rights. SNAP members have been especially outspoken in their protests against bishops and cardinals for their complicity and covering up these acts of clergy sex abuse.

At public demonstrations, these activists carry protest signs aimed at naming and shaming bishops and cardinals who have been involved in cover-ups and who have not reached out to the victim-survivors to offer their own repentance, reparation, and healing care. Besides posters, these protesters on occasions display mementos from the past—religious symbols, now defiled, of sacramental experiences celebrated by victims: children's rosaries, scapulars, first communion photographs, books, and shoes. Often, parents and allies bring pictures of their child or beloved one who has been deeply harmed to these demonstrations.

SNAP has also enacted the compassionate side of prophetic practice as they have held meetings and offered support for those who have been abused. As mentioned, their work has included developing networks of psychologists and lawyers willing to meet with these victim-survivors and their loved ones to provide needed professional care and guidance.

Over its thirty-two years of existence, the prophetic character of this group as a source of resistance, protest, resilience, and accountability has remained intact. At times there have been suspicions and accusations leveled against their relationship with certain lawyers and psychologists who are accused of seeking to capitalize on these tragedies for economic profit and professional advantage. But these challenges have not ultimately undermined the overall effectiveness of the work of this group as a support network and a source of resistance, protest, and a catalyst for transformation of individuals and the challenge to the church.

Allies: Voice of the Faithful

In response to the public revelations about clergy sex abuse by the *Boston Globe* in January 2002, a group of twenty-five practicing Catholics from Wellesley, Massachusetts, gathered at St. John the Evangelist parish to express their anger, their sense of betrayal, and their concern for the church. Many in the group decided to continue to meet weekly to discuss what had given rise to this crisis and how they might respond. Over the weeks that followed, more concerned Catholics joined, and by the spring there were often over seven hundred people attending. An initial core group, comprising professionals, including James Muller, MD, played important roles in launching and naming the group Voice of the Faithful. When the new organization held their first major assembly on July 20th, six months after the first *Globe* article, more than four thousand people were present: "lay people, victims, theologians, priests, and religious from the U.S. and around the world."[8] Currently, VOTF membership exceeds twenty-five thousand from across the United States and worldwide.

Voice of the Faithful and SNAP are quite different organizations. SNAP has always been composed mainly of survivors of clergy sex abuse. They have remained dedicated to two main objectives: first, to offer support for survivors through small group meetings and by helping them find psychological counseling and legal assistance, and second, to protest against suspected abusers and their supervisors. The implications of SNAP's twofold agenda are reflected in their wider mandates: support survivors, protect children, protect the vulnerable, heal the wounded, and expose the truth.

By contrast, the original core of Voice of the Faithful was a group of devoted, active Catholics, many born before or during the Second Vatican Council and its initial implementation. Many of these people have been raised in Catholic families, attended Catholic schools, and have been active in Catholic associations representing a spectrum of spiritualities and charity and social justice orientations. William D'Antonio and Anthony Pogorelc conducted a major sociological analysis of VOTF that discovered that in 2004, over half of its members had been or currently were active in parish and diocesan leadership roles.[9] A significant percentage of VOTF's original membership and leadership were successful professionals with commensurate annual salaries. Reflective of these origins, the organization's membership remains predominately white, relatively affluent, and older, with negligible representation of African Americans, Latinx, and Asian Americans, younger Catholics born after Vatican II, or working-class members.

Given their generational composition, it is not surprising that these concerned Catholics called themselves Voice of the Faithful, and that they self-identified their mission in terms of the motto, "Keep the Faith, Change the Church." Their mission statement is "to provide a prayerful voice, attentive to the Spirit, through which the Faithful can actively participate in the governance of the Catholic Church." This mission is further elaborated by their goals: "to support survivors of clergy sexual abuse; to support priests of integrity; to shape structural change within the Catholic Church."

Besides originally holding weekly meetings in chapters across the United States, VOTF also holds an annual convention whose featured speakers include noteworthy national figures, priests, theologians, and others who have been involved in addressing clerical sexual abuse.

Both SNAP and VOTF are concerned about fostering support and care for survivors of clerical sexual abuse, and both organizations are committed to implementing ecclesial and civic legal accountability for priest-abusers and bishops. However, VOTF's mission statement and goals are more spiritual, theological, and explicitly church centered. The founders of SNAP were influenced by life experiences that included involvement in the Catholic Worker Movement, the feminist spirituality movement, and for some, a history of promoting women's ordination to Catholic priesthood. Barbara Blaine was inspired by Dorothy Day, who did not have a great deal of interest in or patience with Catholic bishops' often narrow understanding of the mission of the church. Although D'Antonio and Pogorelc learned from their surveys and interviews that a significant percentage of VOTF members had, in the past, also been involved in the Catholic Worker or in other expressions of Catholic Action, the mission and goals of the movement were more focused on working within the framework of official Catholic doctrine, canonical structures of participation, and pastoral priorities. Let us identify these.

VOTF declares in their mission statement that through cooperating with the work of the Spirit, reflected in a prayerful voice, they seek to promote the active participation of the faithful in the governance and guidance of the Catholic Church. They commit to advancing this agenda by being "supporters of priests of integrity" and collaborators with bishops, even as they work against clericalism and against bishops who fail to be transparent and accountable. This is indicative of how they seek to "change the Church." It is customary for VOTF conferences and meetings to welcome priests whom they judge to be "of integrity" and to be critics of clerical sexual abuse. They are very insistent that they wish to "keep the faith," the core of the faith, the dogmas of the faith, and that they do not seek to criticize this core or these dogmas or to promote doctrinal development in these areas. They also convey little to no attention to revising canon laws that place limits on how laypeople may participate in the life of the church. For instance, although VOTF's membership seeks greater involvement of laypeople in the selection of bishops, they do not lobby for changing canon law to provide an official role for lay representation in the selection of bishops. Rather, as their policy statements indicate, they work for structural change largely in terms of seeking more robust implementations of the official teachings of Vatican II and the 1983 Code of Canon Law. As we have noted, a significant percentage of VOTF members have served on parish and diocesan committees in the past and are familiar with these forms of lay-clergy collaboration.

VOTF is also not associated with forms of public protest. They are more identified with the development of policy position papers, with support for priests of integrity, advancing nonordained leadership roles for women, calling for married male priests, and requesting a more active (i.e., vocal) role for the laity in the selection of bishops. In an effort to reach out to the wounded victims of clergy abuse, VOTF has promoted restorative justice efforts. These restorative justice efforts have been implemented in the past several decades in various kinds of war-torn areas and other conflict situations, including cases of violent crime in schools and neighborhoods, where they often have gained strong followings and, in many cases, a positive track record. In the case of clerical sex abuse, VOTF acknowledges that restorative justice practices do not take the place of priests being held accountable, both by the church—including being prohibited from practicing priestly ministry—and through legal justice for their criminal behavior. Likewise, restorative justice practices are not a substitute for bishops paying the consequences for their acts of cover-up and practices of secrecy. Questions might be raised, too, about whether restorative justice processes can deal with the deeper and underlying conflictive and controversial issues that contribute to clerical sex abuse and cover-up. Certainly, there is a role for restorative justice practices, but these are not sufficient to address the deeper doctrinal, canonical, and pastoral positions that have influenced these problems.

A major theological question has also been raised about whether the dividing line that VOTF draws between its commitment to work for change in the church, on the one hand, and not advocating change in the faith of the church, on the other, can be as clear cut as its motto, "Keep the Faith—Change the Church," suggests. For example, in order to promote greater lay participation in the selection of bishops and acting against clericalism, mustn't there be a broader consideration of the sanctioned distinction between priests and laity that undergirds the power structure that differentiates the offices, and corresponding duties and rights, of priests and laypeople? Moreover, can the Catholic Church really advance greater participation of women in its decision-making without at least openly discussing women's ordination to the diaconate and priesthood? It seems that VOTF has established a wall between theological and doctrinal development and bureaucratic structural reform, but such a sharp distinction is debatable.

At the same time, as we've seen, VOTF's mission focuses on upholding and fully implementing the teachings of the Second Vatican Council, and this is not an insignificant aim. A church that truly did this would embrace, in practice, the teaching that all of the people of God share in Jesus's prophetic office and shift its policies to take into account the wisdom and sense of faith of the whole community. Still, one has to wonder: absent conflictual acts of protest and calls to change some core ecclesial organizational principles (such as the all-male priesthood and curial-chosen bishops), can VOTF be a genuinely prophetic social movement in the Catholic Church? The constructive change that many VOTF leaders and members are trying to bring about is a more faithful adherence by all the faithful, including clergy and bishops, to the pastoral teachings—especially the lay-empowering teachings—of Vatican II. Yet this approach presses for no structural change, but only to "implement" Vatican II and the 1983 Code of Canon Law.

Is, then, SNAP prophetic, while VOTF is not? Or do we have here two different styles of prophecy? With VOTF members, Catholic survivors who are members of SNAP would affirm Vatican II's teaching on the laity's sharing in Jesus's prophetic missions. And yet SNAP members embrace a more radical prophetic style, recognizing the need for protest movements and conflictive approaches in order to promote communal discernment of systemic changes. In SNAP, we see a prophetic style in the spirit of Amos in the Hebrew Bible and in the style of Jesus of Nazareth in those gospel traditions that show him in conflict with certain expressions of his own Jewish faith (both rigorist and lax) and with economically and politically exclusionary practices of the Roman Empire. Perhaps one could, by contrast, envision VOTF's prophetic style in the spirit of the priestly identified Ezekiel or Jeremiah, or Jesus who routinely participated in his Jewish tradition while seeking to reform it from within, making it truer to what it proclaimed.

Witnesses:
Investigative Journalists

Investigative journalists can also be described as functioning as prophetic witnesses insofar as they search for victims of abuse caught in deeper institutional networks of power, revealing patterns of injustice that cry out for attention. In so doing, journalists and other contributors to public media play a particular, and important, prophetic role in civil society and in some instances in the church—even though they themselves might not understand their role as prophetic in this way, and certain Catholic critics would dismiss any such comparison.

To suggest that there might be something like a prophetic motivation and function served by investigative reporting is not to dismiss reasonable debates about the limitations or flaws that specific reports may contain. It is not uncommon for religious spokespersons to decry such reporting in the secular press as seeking to discredit the authority of the Catholic Church, or of any religious tradition in modern society. Most respondents to such critiques situate their debate within the larger discussion about the role of the press in uncovering the truth, and in drawing attention to victims and the marginalized in the defense of freedom and democracy. It is neither customary nor, on the face of it, convincing, to defend such reporters by arguing they are prophetic.[10]

Nevertheless, it is worth considering the prophetic character of the work of investigative reporters and other journalists in exposing clergy sex abuse in the Catholic Church. It is not surprising that some reporters who have written on this subject have also been victims of abuse or have had close personal relationships with abused individuals; these undercurrents have shaped their identities and animate their witness. Out of many possible examples, we will examine two instances of investigative reporting to assess their prophetic role.

There have been numerous noteworthy investigative reports across the United States of clerical sex abuse of minors since May 1985, when Jason Berry first reported on priest-abuser Gilbert Gauthe in the *Times of Acadiane* in Lafayette, Louisiana.[11] The *Boston Globe*, however, initiated an entirely new phase of reporting on this subject when, between May 1992 and December 1993, the paper published sixty-five articles on the case of James Porter, who had abused approximately one hundred boys and girls. But no other news reports are comparable in breadth and depth to the subsequent work, almost a decade later, of the *Boston Globe* Spotlight Investigative Team, initially composed of three reporters, Matt Carroll, Sacha Pfeiffer, and Michael Rezendes, and their editor, Walter V. Robinson, who began in August 2001 to research the sexual abuse of children by clergy in the Boston area and to ask how much church officials had known about these events.

Through contact with lawyers, public court records, victim support groups, and publicly available sources such as the church's annual directories, the reporters identified and established a pernicious pattern. Accused priests were reassigned and court settlements reached, complete with confidentiality agreements and sealed court records to protect the church from unwanted publicity about these matters and, at least purportedly, to protect victims from the glare of public attention. Pieces of the puzzle started to come together.[12]

Among the many cases of clergy child sexual abuse identified by these reporters, the most notorious figure was John Geoghan.

Geoghan engaged in multiple incidents of abuse during six parish assignments beginning in 1967 and stretching across thirty-four years, including after Bernard Law became archbishop of Boston in 1984. In its 2002 series, the Spotlight team gave special attention to Geoghan's history, which at that point had led to over 130 accusations and 84 civil lawsuits. Beyond Geoghan's criminal conduct, the Spotlight team was also intent on discovering how Cardinal Law had dealt with these cases, and their research showed that he had engaged in widespread practices of secrecy and cover-up. In doing their jobs as journalists to bring Boston's clergy abuse scandal into public view, the Spotlight investigative team performed the crucial prophetic functions of listening to the laments of victims of sex abuse, then giving voice to the voiceless and powerless. In using their secular newspaper to challenge powerful religious authorities, they thereby acted as a prophetic witness.

Father Geoghan and Cardinal Law were the focus of the first set of reports that appeared in the *Globe* on January 6 and 7, 2002. These reports detailed the nature and extent of Geoghan's abusive behavior and the diverse victims involved. They also revealed the knowledge that Cardinal Law had of Geoghan's behavior and Law's responsibility for repeatedly moving him from parish to parish after sexual transgressions occurred. One heartbreaking story, published on the series' first day, featured a grieving mother of seven boys, Maryette Dussourd. The piece recounted this mother's terrible guilt for failing to recognize Geoghan's grooming methods in seeking out a mother who had her hands full with childcare, and him forming relationships with and then taking inappropriate interest in her children. At a certain point he began to put the boys to bed, bathe them, read to them, and over time begin to engage in sexual activities. The January 7th feature story again focused on Geoghan, with the title "Geoghan Preferred Preying on Poorer Children." Besides confronting them with dramatic and disturbing illustrations of clergy abuse of children, the *Globe* stories further incited their readers' justifiable anger by revealing the church's abject ineffectiveness in addressing these situations.

By the end of the Spotlight series' first month in print, two basic breakthroughs took place. First, the team, which had been gathering information about instances of abuse by other priests, published an initial report on what they were finding in their January 31, 2002 article, "Scores of Priests Involved in Sex Abuse Cases." On a second front, the *Globe* had been inundated with new information made available by newly unsealed court documents in the Geoghan case. In August 2001, lawyers for the *Globe* had petitioned that Geoghan's history of court proceedings and settlements be unsealed in the public interest. In November, Superior Court Judge Constance Sweeney, who was raised Catholic and educated at Catholic institutions, supported the *Globe* and ruled to unseal the documents. After an appeal, the documents were unsealed shortly after the *Globe* began publishing its series.

On February 24th two further reports were published. One was on the more than two hundred people who had contacted lawyers after the initial stories appeared, and the possibility that this number could expand to three hundred or more. Others had gone to the archdiocese instead of to a lawyer to make a complaint. The second report addressed the "church cloaked in a culture of silence." Pastors and priests and other church administrators who knew about these accusations, proven or not, were discouraged from speaking to individuals or groups in the parish about cases of abuse.

The *Globe*'s findings showed how the bishops' individual and collective choices perpetuated a culture of secrecy and cover-up. But more importantly, it revealed horrible dysfunction not only among some priests and bishops, but also in core church structures associated with the exercise of power, the use of money, and the understanding—or denial—of the unchecked extent of clerical and episcopal authority. In the wake of all this, the church's reputation and functioning would not be recovered easily, if at all.

What the *Globe* described as "a legal watershed" was reported on May 12, 2002, with the title "Scandal Erodes Traditional Deference to Church." The story described Judge Constance M. Sweeney "order[ing] Cardinal Bernard F. Law to submit to questioning by lawyers for the alleged victims of convicted pedophile and defrocked priest John J. Gallagher last week." A cardinal, the reporters noted, had never before been "forced to submit to the standards of the secular world in the most Catholic metropolitan area in the nation," so in Boston the incident represented both "a cultural change and a legal one." The story discussed what this shift meant for Attorney General Thomas F. Reilly, attorney Kevin M. Burke, and five other district attorneys covering areas within the archdiocese, all of them Catholic. These lawyers were urged by their fellow Catholics to be tougher.

The final stories of 2002 narrated the last scenes in this act of the Boston clergy abuse drama. The first, published on December 1, was on Cardinal Law being forced to consider bankruptcy in the midst of the financial disaster that resulted from court verdicts against the Archdiocese of Boston, with a second article recounting the ongoing legal efforts to gain access to sealed court files covering over two hundred cases. A few days later there was another story about David Clohessy, the executive director of SNAP at the time, who joined other victims in a public protest urging that more files be released. On December 10, a report appeared about fifty-eight priests urging Cardinal Law to resign. And on December 14, the *Globe* printed a picture of Law meeting with John Paul II, a meeting in which the pope accepted Law's resignation.

What makes investigative reporters, when they do their jobs with integrity, like prophets? They often have a reputation as muckrakers, interested only in bringing to light the bad side of powerful people, including well-respected people, especially with salacious stories. It is not uncommon for reporters to be accused of using slander, innuendo, and falsehoods to discredit someone's reputation. And as already mentioned, the secular press in general is frequently accused of negative bias in its reporting on religious leaders and institutions.

When it comes to the treatment of religion by reporters, not all investigative reporters are against religion, and some reporters adhere to religious traditions and practices. Certainly, there are instances when charges against journalists of antireligious bias hold water. Yet on balance, many investigative journalists are genuinely interested in and committed to uncovering the truth and then speaking truth to power, especially corrupt power. This is a virtue of investigative reporting shared by classic prophets intent on unmasking hypocrisy. In the Hebrew Bible prophets had the courage of their convictions to criticize priests and their minions, and kings and their royal courts who desecrated the honor due to God and violated the dignity due to God's children by failing to care for the poor, the marginalized, children, and the vulnerable. Jesus is portrayed in the Gospels as a prophet in this tradition who speaks truth to power and stands firmly against injustice and religious hypocrisy.

For the sake of brevity, I have focused here on the prophetic witness of the Spotlight reporters in the case of sexual abuse of minors in Boston. But journalists have also been involved in uncovering other forms of abuse and dysfunction. In December 2002, for example, Sacha Pfeiffer wrote in the *Globe* about adult female victims of clergy abuse. This kind of story, including cases of clergy abuse of women religious, has received relatively little attention thus far. Reporters have also increasingly been asking challenging questions of powerful people in public. Nicole Winfield from the Associated Press, for instance, asked Pope Francis during a press conference on February 5, 2019, whether the Vatican has acknowledged and is pursuing clerical sexual abuse of women religious.[13] In response, the pope acknowledged this situation in public, which is the first time a pope or papal officials has made such an admission, beginning by saying, "There have been priests, and even bishops, who have done that," and "We have been working on this for some time."

Advocates and Arbiters of Justice: Grand Juries

The Pennsylvania Grand Jury Report released on August 14, 2018, received considerable attention for its searing critique of the institutional failure of the Catholic Church to protect minors against the criminal behavior of clergy and of the many Catholic bishops in the state who had covered up clergy sexual abuse in their respective dioceses. Not since the series of *Boston Globe* reports in 2001 had so much public attention been given to clergy abuse. Even though there have only been a relatively small number of such reports issued by grand juries and state attorneys general, notably in Maine, Massachusetts, New Hampshire, and Pennsylvania, grand juries have become recognized as advocates for victim-survivors in their quest for justice. These grand jury reports can present compelling evidence and render strong judgments against purportedly offending clergy and bishops, but they are not without their critics, as we shall see.

It is helpful to situate the efforts of grand juries in the larger context of two other basic ways in which people seek to redress Catholic clergy sex abuse of minors through the U.S. legal system. One legal procedure available to sexual abuse victim-survivors is called a tort lawsuit, also called a civil lawsuit, that is used when a civil tort, that is a harmful wrong, takes place against an individual or more than one. The abuse victims, the plaintiffs, and the accused abuser, the defendant, can choose to have a trial by jury, and often do, but they could request the case be decided by a judge alone. In tort lawsuits the focus is on compensating the victim for damages incurred by wrongful acts, and the civil burden of proof in such cases is a preponderance of evidence. A criminal lawsuit provides a second avenue in which the objective is to consider whether the defendant should be punished for committing a crime, and the required burden of proof is that the case must be made beyond a reasonable doubt.

In civil lawsuits, someone who has been abused or their representative makes an accusation of one or more claims, or cause(s) of action, that is, violations of the law, against an alleged clergy abuser or multiple abusers, in which case not all claims would necessarily apply to more than one defendant. The plaintiff can make a claim against the defendant, the individual priest, but a claim can also be made against the employer, that is, the institution where the accused clergy exercises his ministry, which may be a parish, diocese, school, or religious order, or more than one of these. A plaintiff could be successful in proving their case, but the accused priest may have no assets, and therefore the accuser receives no money for damages, but this is why the plaintiff regularly makes a claim against the employer as well. The claims against the clergy could include assault, battery, and infliction of emotional distress, whereas an institution can be accused of being negligent of supervision and retention, or of vicarious liability.[14] There have been thousands of these civil lawsuits in allegations of clergy sex abuse in the United States.

Grand jury reports provide a third avenue for legally addressing clergy sexual abuse, which is a criminal procedure undertaken by state attorneys general, local district attorneys, or, though only rarely, by a U.S. attorney general. Grand juries are distinct from trial juries, which are most commonly used in cases of clergy sex abuse. Trial juries are used at criminal and civil proceedings, which are based on accusations by individual plaintiffs (the victims) against a defendant (an accused clergyman, diocesan administrator, or bishop). In either form of trial jury, civil or criminal, the defendant can appear in court, testify in their own defense, and have witnesses called to support their defense. These proceedings are adversarial—only one side can win—but they often end in settlements or agreements without a verdict being rendered. Many victims find these legal proceedings to be difficult if not traumatic, and they often result in no clear admission by the accused that they have committed a crime. Furthermore, statutes of limitations in various jurisdictions have prevented many older sexual abuse cases from being tried in either criminal or civil court.

BishopAccountability.org, an online public ombudsman, reports that allegations have been made against 6,721 Catholic priests and 19 bishops between 1950 and 2016; additionally, many more names of alleged priests and bishops have been released by dioceses and religious institutes in the United States since 2017.[15] BishopAccountability.org further reports that over $3 billion has been paid out in awards and settlements in cases of clergy sexual abuse of minors.

In other cases, an attorney general can determine that a grand jury should be convened to address a particular form of legal violation that merits attention.[16] A grand jury is composed of sixteen to twenty-three members and only a simple majority is needed when reaching a decision. Grand juries do not reach a decision about the guilt or innocence of a defendant, as occurs in civil actions or criminal trials. Instead, a grand jury hears evidence and deliberates without any defense attorneys (*ex parte*) raising questions or making a case on behalf of the defendants. The aim of the grand jury is to determine whether there is probable cause, which need not be established beyond a reasonable doubt, to address an institutional failure or to indict a defendant for a crime. If the grand jury rules in the affirmative, the case will then be considered by a trial jury, with both prosecuting and defending attorneys presenting evidence, witnesses, and arguments in an adversarial fashion. Because protections for potential defendants are less stringent than in a trial, grand jury proceedings can address older cases and cases where there might appear to be insufficient evidence for a conviction.

Between 2002 and 2018, eight grand jury reports on the clerical sexual abuse of minors in the United States were issued;[17] other grand juries were impaneled during this time but had issued no final reports.[18] Since 2018, a number of additional state attorneys general have been gathering information from the public about previously unknown abuse cases, as they consider whether to pursue this legal proceeding.[19]

Members of a grand jury serve as advocates of justice in cases of clergy sexual abuse of minors in a manner comparable to prophetic forms of discourse when they issue indictments or denunciations of injustices that require forms of institutional reform or reparation.[20] As of 2020, no grand jury has legally indicted a bishop for his role in clerical sexual abuse of minors and ordered the state to proceed to a criminal trial against him.[21] Rather, many of these reports have served as summations of available evidence. In cases of clergy sexual abuse of minors, grand juries prepare an investigative report based on the evidence, testimonies, and arguments that have been presented to them. In so doing, grand juries have certain advantages, even when they do not lead to criminal charges. First, a grand jury report can bring to light an institution's failures to respect the rights of those in their care. Second, a grand jury can legally compel the disclosure of evidence, such as official documents, including personnel evaluations of accused clergy and diocesan records pertaining to ministerial placements,

letters between a bishop and priests in his diocese, or other pertinent materials. Third, a grand jury can insist upon the testimony
of reticent witnesses, such as bishops, who have information relevant to the jury's evaluation of the legal conduct of the institution
involved—in these cases, diocese(s) and religious order(s).

In cases of clerical sexual abuse of minors, along with consulting documentary evidence, grand juries customarily receive
testimony from bishops, victims, and psychological professionals.
This procedure can bring to light information that has been intentionally withheld, and arguments can be made that certain institutional practices should be reformed in order to address these
situations. The grand jury can also function as a promoter or arbiter of justice by ascertaining laws that merit amendment or nul-
lification and by rendering official recommendations. By acting as
advocates for and arbiters of justice, grand juries fulfill particular
prophetic functions in civil society even though they are not trial
juries or judges.

A number of grand juries that have considered cases of clergy
sexual abuse and episcopal malfeasance have come up with similar legislative recommendations. These include the following:
first, eliminate or extend the statute of limitations in cases of clerical sexual abuse of minors, in light of delays in reporting caused
by repressed memories or debilitating shame and guilt over the
abuse; second, implement mandatory reporting to civil authorities by priests, bishops, and religious superiors in cases of clerical
sexual abuse of minors; and third, annul and prohibit confidentiality agreement settlements in cases of clergy sexual abuse and
misconduct.[22]

Attorneys general and grand juries have been called to give
voice on behalf of victims of injustice and the powerless against
corrupt and powerful individuals in society and in religious institutions. Again, these are traits that are traditionally associated
with prophets, who act as advocates for the vulnerable and render
judgments against corrupt religious and political leaders. In certain cases, biblical prophets were recognized for being affiliated
with the priestly caste or as advisors to royal authorities. Similarly,
attorneys general and grand juries have civil and legal authority

in taking their public stances against religious authorities in cases involving allegedly corrupt and hypocritical leaders who have mishandled and concealed the sexual abuse of minors by clergy.

Based on all that has been disclosed through the media and through the work of such groups as SNAP and BishopAccountability .org, bishops today have often been judged by the wider public to be unreliable and irresponsible sources of information about clergy sex abuse. Grand juries, however, have been considered more authoritative in civil society and, in some ways more than victims, allies, and reporters, trustworthy agents for reporting and challenging the behavior of priests, bishops, and the exercise of power and authority in the church. Consequently, journalists often treat grand jury reports as particularly reliable sources of information when advancing a story of sex abuse by clergy.[23]

Cathleen Kaveny, a professor of law, ethics, and theology, has written about the role of prophetic discourse in civic society in the United States and particularly the role of the *jeremiad*, a form of prophetic indictment of evil and injustice that draws on the rhetorical forms associated with the classic prophets in the Hebrew Scriptures: Amos, Hosea, Jeremiah, and Isaiah.[24] Her argument is consistent with my earlier emphasis on the important role of heeding lamentations in prophetic discourse and corroborates Kaveny's attention to the rhetorical structure of prophetic indictment in political, legal, and ecclesial settings. Her concluding argument has particular relevance in this section. She claims that prophetic indictments associated with the jeremiad need to be tempered with compassionate and humble truth telling, which she finds illustrated biblically in the use of irony in the prophetic Book of Jonah. As the title of her book indicates, in political as in juridical discourse there should be *Prophecy without Contempt*. Kaveny's claim here is important to keep in mind when assessing grand jury reports on clergy sexual abuse of minors and the uses to which these reports may be put in the media and in popular opinion.

If we examine all of the currently available grand jury reports pertaining to clerical sexual abuse of minors, we will find, I suggest, that they are all making prophetic indictments of the failures of ecclesial institutions, bishops, and clergy to live up to their institutional mission, especially as it bears upon the care and protection of children. Yet in these reports, one also finds a number of different styles operative. Some are formal in tone. Their presentation of the case, treatment of the evidence, and conclusions reflect a style of emotionally detached precision and respect for both the victim-survivors and the bishops and clergy being judged, even when a resolutely negative assessment is being made. By contrast, the discourse of other grand jury reports—the 2018 Pennsylvania Grand Jury Report offers a clear example—is passionate, one might argue vitriolic and, using Kaveny's words, "contemptuous" about the bishops' actions, if not about the bishops themselves.

As morally corrupt as the behavior of bishops and systemic institutional practices being criticized have surely been, one can ask whether such an incendiary form of rhetoric fans the flames of panic rather than sparking action for repair and needed change. Does such a style of rhetoric, regardless of the substance of the denunciation, best serve civil society and the fundamental institutional reform that is needed? To put the matter differently, can a grand jury advance an agonistic accusation in the interest of justice without fostering contempt? Though not an easy task, I believe that it can, and grand juries ought to aim to do so.

Some observers have offered thoughtful critiques of recent grand jury reports and their coverage by the media, attempting to reframe certain issues involved. One such attempt has been submitted by longtime *New York Times* reporter Peter Steinfels, who has offered a substantive critique of the Pennsylvania Grand Jury Report for failing to reasonably consider the historical context and time lag between the events of abuse, the legal accusations, and the grand jury report itself. More importantly, Steinfels criticizes this report for not taking into consideration the remedial efforts taken by certain bishops to address the mistakes they have made, associated with the actions taken by the collective body of U.S. Bishops. These are issues that merit further attention, and we will return to them in our next chapter.[25]

Conclusion

Certain bishops, clergy, and laypeople have viewed the various voices, protests, and movements treated in this chapter as outsiders, peripheral expressions, and overly shrill prophetic denunciations of the Catholic Church and its ordained leaders. Too often, those who have promoted accountability, transparency, and responsibility by bishops in the matter of clergy of sexual abuse of young people have been marginalized, criticized, and had their motives questioned. However, instead of casting these prophetic utterances as extrinsic efforts that are illegitimate and contrary to the identity and mission of the church, the deeper and more challenging question is this: How can these voices, protests, and movements be internalized as authentic expressions of the prophetic office of all the faithful, including the laity among the people of God?

Chapter 4

The Responses of Bishops

The prophetic denunciations covered in the last chapter call for radical and fundamental change in the church. We will consider this claim from a much wider perspective in chapter 5, but in this chapter, I want to look more carefully at bishops' responses to the clergy abuse scandal, taking as my cue a line of argument advanced by Catholic historian and distinguished religion journalist Peter Steinfels in response to the 2018 Pennsylvania Grand Jury Report. In a lengthy article published on January 25, 2019, Steinfels took an unpopular position by offering a careful, substantive critique of this report. While fully acknowledging the horrors of its subject matter, Steinfels argued that the report failed to take adequately into account the historical contexts of and the time lags between the events of the abuse, the legal accusations, and the grand jury report itself. More importantly, he criticized the report for not taking into consideration the remedial efforts that had been taken by certain bishops, but also in noteworthy ways by the collective body of U.S. Bishops. While his more nuanced approach went against the grain of many in the media and public anger that the report had evoked, he raises issues that merit further attention.[1]

When we ask how "the church" thinks about and handles controversy, we have to first ask what we mean by "the church." "The church" can be used to identify all Christians, regardless of their particular confessional tradition, such as Orthodox, Anglican,

Lutheran, Presbyterian, Methodist, Baptist, or Pentecostal. Catholics in the past and, to a certain extent, even now have tended to think about "the church" as an institution and the administrative structure that governs it: the pope, the central bureaucracy identified as the Roman curia; the priests, bishops, archbishops, and cardinals of particular dioceses and archdioceses; and their various administrators and employees. The church can also identify all baptized Catholics. In the previous chapter, we considered how several groups of prophetic laypeople, both inside and outside the Catholic Church, have analyzed and responded to the clergy sex abuse controversy. We have also seen glimpses of how the U.S. Bishops generally acted, from the 1970s to the present, and considered in depth how three successive popes have spoken about the root cause of the crisis. This chapter will take a closer look at some of the history of the bishops' responses to this controversy.

Survivors, their allies, media witnesses, legal advocates, and most U.S. Catholics, as well as people across the religious and political spectrum in the United States and around the world, have all expressed their anger at the criminal behavior of offending clergy. But they have conveyed special acrimony toward bishops whose policies and practices contributed to the suffering of the survivors. Newspapers, TV documentaries, books, and movies have chronicled how some bishops failed victims and their communities of support. Frequently bishops have been vilified, in many cases not without reason. All too often these men did not reach out to victims and their loved ones to listen to, learn from, and support them. Bishops often seemed more concerned about the accused priests' psychological well-being, about the risk of "scandal," and about the financial viability of the local church than they did about the physical and psychological damage done to survivors and communities. Bishops' reputations were further sullied by reports of millions of dollars being spent on fighting against extending or waiving statutes of limitations to protect the assets of the church from lawsuits by the abused. Not surprisingly, many Catholic laypeople, frustrated with the failure of the church to hold its senior officials accountable, have lost their confidence in the decisions taken by bishops, not only on this issue but in other areas as well.[2] But is it fair to say that the bishops did nothing?

In fact, some individual bishops and groups of bishops did try to be responsive to the accusations made against priests in their dioceses. This chapter will analyze some of the most important constructive efforts made by U.S. bishops as well as by the three most recent bishops of Rome—John Paul II, Benedict XVI, and Francis. You might, in view of their collective record, be inclined to reject or to be skeptical about the value of these leaders' responses. But given their power in the church, if we are to fairly and critically assess their record, it is important to understand what bishops and popes did do to address the problem of clergy abuse, and why. To do this we must consider both the personal qualities of various bishops, and the changing historical context within which they made individual and collective decisions.

Disparate Reactions before 2001

As increasing numbers of instances of clergy abuse of young people came to their attention, many bishops initially felt overwhelmed, as they were left on their own to address these complex issues in relative isolation.[3] As we have seen, the U.S. Bishops first confronted rising incidents and reports of clergy sex abuse amid the tumultuous aftermath of the Second Vatican Council. At that time, in the late 1960s and early 1970s, the U.S. and Latin American bishops were in the initial phases of implementing processes of decentralized discernment and decision-making in the church, above all through the promotion of the collegiality of bishops at episcopal conferences. Some U.S. bishops also advanced the participation of laypeople in parish ministries, parish and diocesan councils, and diocesan synods.[4] This was a time, in the late 1960s and early '70s, when instances of clergy sexual abuse were escalating dramatically. Yet it was not until the early '90s, after the Gilbert Gauthe cases received increasing national attention, that a flurry of reports of abuse was received. However, it was not until after the

Boston Globe Spotlight reports began to appear in 2002 that the number of cases of abuse skyrocketed.

The John Jay Report provided information about the early public responses of the U.S. Bishops to clergy sex abuse of minors. The John Jay team also gathered data from diocesan surveys about bishops' initial responses in cases of priests accused of sexually abusing children and analyzed that data using organization theory and other social scientific methods.[5] Accused priests were variously "reprimanded and returned" to ministry; "referred for evaluation"; "given administrative leave"; they "resigned or retired"; were "suspended"; or "no further action was taken."[6]

Behind the range of actions catalogued by John Jay investigators were bishops who often felt, and indeed were, ill-equipped to engage young victims of abuse or their parents and families. Only rarely did a bishop have any training in the effects of this kind of behavior on children. They were also ill-prepared to handle rising cases of litigation against accused priests and the church, and the accompanying risks of financial loss. In attempting to legally protect the church, civil lawyers usually advised bishops not to speak with the abused or their parents, guardians, or lawyers. Bishops were urged to prioritize their churches' legal and financial protection at the expense of their pastoral and human responsibilities to abused congregants and their families. One bishop told of contacting the highly respected Cardinal Joseph Bernardin of Chicago to ask his advice about following his lawyers' counsel in this regard. Bernardin counseled the bishop not to follow the recommendation of the lawyers, but to be pastoral. Even though this kind of strategy might have costly repercussions, Bernardin told the bishop, it was the right thing to do. Yet many bishops, as we have seen, did follow their lawyers' advice and avoided admitting any wrongdoing by their priests, even in pastoral conversations with victims and their families.[7]

U.S. Bishops began to face the public crisis of clergy sex abuse during the papacy of John Paul II. Elected in 1978, John Paul II advanced a renewed policy of centralization in the church, with greater emphasis on the teaching authority of the pope and on the role of the Vatican curia in promoting adherence to papal teaching and policies. With Cardinal Joseph Ratzinger, whom he chose to be in charge of the Congregation for the Doctrine of the Faith, Pope John Paul II challenged the U.S. Bishops' recent exercises of decentralized and collaborative methods of learning and teaching through their National Conference of Catholic Bishops (NCCB). And when U.S. Bishops retired, John Paul II consistently chose replacements who supported and would implement his centralized style of exercising power and authority. Whether appointed as bishops by John Paul II or by his predecessors, the U.S. Bishops faced a very steep learning curve as they confronted revelations of clergy abuse of minors, especially beginning in 1984, when Gilbert Gauthe's record as a serial abuser received widespread public attention, and subsequently as reporting of previous incidents of abuse by other priests during the 1960s and 1970s began to rise sharply.

To describe and analyze the various ways bishops responded to this unprecedented and evolving situation, the John Jay Report used categories drawn from an influential 1962 book by sociologist Everett M. Rogers, *The Diffusion of Innovations*.[8] Bishops were required to learn a great deal about clergy sexual abuse beginning in the mid-1980s and throughout the 1990s, an education they received through lived experiences in their dioceses but also through written reports, committee work, and by gathering information about sexual abuse through a variety of sources, often from secular media.

Rogers identified various ways that people adapt to change and unfamiliar new situations, and John Jay experts specified four as particularly relevant for the work of the bishops. (1) Some made their decisions by weighing the relative advantages to the victims and their parents in relation to risk of scandal and damages to the church. (2) Others privileged commitment to tradition, continuity, and stability, over innovations to address problems and needs. (3) There were those who resisted or slowly implemented changes based on group decision-making with people, especially laypeople, with a different level of status and authority, in the interest of promoting accountability. (4) When certain bishops failed to understand the long-term value of transparency and open communication, they resisted change.[9]

The bishops' first tentative effort to address the problem collectively came in June 1985, when the National Conference of Catholic

Bishops, renamed in 2001 the United States Conference of Catholic Bishops (USCCB), met to address the fallout from the Gauthe case. In advance of this meeting a confidential manual was prepared and circulated to the bishops who would be in attendance. Cowritten by Thomas Doyle, a priest and canon lawyer; Michael Peterson, a priest and psychiatrist; and Raymond Mouton, a layperson and civil lawyer, the document was entitled "The Problem of Sexual Molestation by Roman Catholic Clergy: Meeting the Problem in a Comprehensive and Responsible Manner."[10] Its aim was to help the U.S. Bishops as they responded to clergy abuse and its multifaceted dimensions and implications pertaining to civil law, criminal law, clinical and medical factors, canon law, insurance, spiritual matters, and public relations. The document proposed that a group of four bishops trained in canon law and civil law be selected to develop a comprehensive approach to the problem. This group, in turn, was to identify two other groups of experts—a Crisis Control Team and a Policy and Planning Team. But Doyle, Mouton, and Peterson's proposal was rejected by the U.S. Bishops' Conference without any explanation as to why.[11] The failure of the bishops to adopt this proposal, regardless of the reasons, came to represent a symbol of ongoing apprehension, resistance, and long-standing rejection of taking responsibility by individual bishops from the National Conference of Catholic Bishops in the matter of clergy sex abuse and episcopal concealment.

Three years later, in 1988, the General Council of the NCCB, which works with the organization's president and other officers as the governing oversight council of the episcopal conference, issued a public statement setting forth several courses of action dioceses might take in cases of sexual abuse. These were then standardized, discussed at subsequent national meetings, and released in 1992 as the "Five Principles" that bishops were to follow in response to accusations of abuse.[12] According to these principles, all dioceses were to

1. Respond promptly to all credible allegations
2. In cases with sufficient evidence, relieve the alleged offender promptly of ministerial duties and recommend appropriate medical evaluation and psychological intervention

3. Comply with duties of civil law on incident reporting and cooperate with investigation
4. Reach out to victims and families with a commitment to their spiritual and emotional well-being
5. Within the confines of respect for the privacy of the individuals involved, deal as openly as possible with the members of the community

These initial steps toward devising a common approach to the crisis would be followed by other strategic responses developed over the next three decades. With every step advanced there were bishops eager to follow the new policies, but there were also those who resisted. The John Jay investigators discussed a range of examples where individual bishops stood during the 1990s and into the new millennium on the implementation of the Five Principles, using sociologist Everett Rogers's categories for different cohorts of responders to change: "innovators, earlier adopters, early majority, later majority, and laggards."[13] Among the bishops, John Jay researchers found numerous laggards, as well as consternation and manifestations of resistance.

After the promulgation of the Five Principles in 1992, sub-committees of the NCCB undertook a series of efforts to aid the bishops. First, in 1992 Father Canice Connors was appointed the chairman of the Priestly Life and Ministry subcommittee on sexual abuse by priests. This group developed, and in 1993 ran, a two-day, expert-led workshop for church leaders on clergy abuse of minors they called the Think Tank. During 1993 the Bishops' Ad Hoc Committee on Sexual Abuse was also established. Chaired by Bishop John F. Kinney, this committee implemented a survey on clergy sexual abuse that was completed by thirty-two (roughly a third of the) U.S. dioceses and archdioceses. Survey results revealed that more than half of the responding dioceses were reassigning offending priests who had undergone some form of treatment back into parish ministries.[14] Bishop Kinney's committee questioned this practice, and in particular urged bishops to remove priests with "enduring attraction to children" from active ministry. Based on the Ad Hoc Committee's findings and recommendations, Think Tank organizers elaborated further on the Five Principles in a two-part manual, *Restoring Trust*, which was distributed to all bishops in 1994.

From its inception in 1993 through the landmark meeting of the bishops in Dallas in 2002, the Ad Hoc Committee on Clergy Sexual Abuse played a crucial role in helping U.S. Bishops and members of dioceses become better educated and more active in responding to what was transpiring in parishes, schools, and diocesan offices. They monitored the implementation of sexual abuse policies, established review boards to consider accusations against priests, and developed evaluations of candidates for ordination and staff training. This committee proactively promoted education on clergy sexual abuse, a quick response time to victims and their families, placing accused priests on leave, removing "credibly accused priests" from ministry with children, and cooperating with media without revealing names of victims and priests.[15] Bishops' initial feelings of unpreparedness and isolation were ameliorated to some degree because of the work of this Ad Hoc Committee. By the end of the millennium the national body of bishops, and many dioceses, had made advances in developing sexual abuse policies, creating review boards that included lay members, and adopting requirements for mandatory reporting of abuse.

The Dallas Charter in 2002

The *Boston Globe* Spotlight reports that began appearing in 2002 made it clear that many incidents of clergy sexual abuse that were only then being reported had in fact taken place ten, twenty, or more years earlier. After a decade of the U.S. Bishops' efforts to implement policies and procedures for addressing clergy sexual abuse of minors, the Spotlight revelations left the bishops in the U.S. and officials in the Vatican deeply shaken at the extent of the problem. In Boston, both prior to and in the wake of the Spotlight reports, Cardinal Bernard Law provided a horrifying example of what bishops should not do in the face of incidents of clergy sex abuse. The revulsion of Catholics and the wider public and the anger elicited by the *Globe*'s revelations of individual priests' crimes were compounded immensely by institutional failures to address abusive behavior that the newspaper uncovered.

It had become abundantly clear that the bishops needed to address the clergy abuse scandal at deeper levels and in more comprehensive and effective ways. When, in June 2002, the USCCB met in Dallas, they had the urgent task of responding to the public and ecclesial crisis. This meeting elicited substantive collegial action by the U.S. Bishops. That gathering did not simply result in individual bishops offering their own diocesan responses, nor in an ugly expression of a fragmented and polarized group of bishops. Instead, the bishops at Dallas advanced collective responses, responses that were substantive despite their deficiencies.

The most important action developed to date in response to clergy sexual abuse, then, was approved collectively by the U.S. Bishops five months after the *Boston Globe* series began in January. The bishops approved a Charter for the Protection of Children and Young People along with "Essential Norms," a document that established canonical legal requirements. Crafted as a commitment or pledge between the bishops and the faithful in the United States, the Charter built upon and expanded both the Five Principles approved in 1992 and 1993's *Restoring Trust*. The Charter was crafted with the intention of communicating effectively to a U.S. Catholic audience. Its sequence of the promises, which were called articles, aimed to advance a compelling rhetorical argument.[16]

The bishops begin by expressing the church's primary commitment to the care and healing of victim/survivors and their families (no. 1). Subsequent articles lay out specific policies and practices required of all dioceses. Among these: Dioceses must have policies, procedures, and trained personnel for meeting with survivors and those accompanying them. In addition, dioceses must establish review boards to provide confidential assessments for the bishop about each abuse case, to ensure that allegations are thoroughly investigated and to offer advice about whether the priest should be removed from ministry during that investigation (no. 2). The Charter repudiates confidentiality agreements with victims-survivors, unless there are special reasons raised by the victim-survivor (no. 3). Every accusation brought to the attention of the office of the bishop is to be reported to civil authorities (no. 4). If a priest or deacon is proven to have engaged in "a single act of sexual abuse," he will be permanently removed from ministry and from priesthood if warranted. The secular media used the expression "a zero-tolerance policy" to describe this commitment by the bishops (no. 5). Standards for ministerial behavior with children and young people are to be established (no. 6). Each diocese will develop policies of transparency and openness (no. 7).

The Charter also made moves to institutionalize the bishops' commitments, establishing a national Secretariat, or Office, for Child and Youth Protection, to be staffed with trained professionals that would assist dioceses in "implementing 'safe environment' programs," create auditing procedures to assure compliance, and prepare an annual report on program implementation (no. 8). It also created a National Review Board, to be made up of laypeople, to assist the president of the USCCB in reviewing the Secretariat's annual reports on local dioceses, and to advise the president of the USCCB on policies and practices (no. 9). To reinforce the Charter's promises and create accountability for their implementation, the bishops approved an accompanying statement linking the articles to canonical (church) legal norms. Subsequently, the two documents were formally received and the Norms legally recognized by the appropriate officials of the Roman curia.

Since their original release in 2002, the Charter Promises and the Essential Norms have been subjected to a range of criticisms and proposals for revision, both by bishops and by advocacy groups such as BishopAccountability.org. For instance, the original version of Norm 8 states, "When even a single act of sexual abuse by a priest or deacon is admitted or is established after an appropriate process in accord with canon law, the offending priest or deacon will be removed permanently from ecclesiastical ministry, not excluding dismissal from the clerical state, if the case so warrants"; but critics found "an appropriate process" too open-ended and insufficient to hold clergy or bishops accountable. But critics' most repeated complaint has been that the Norms offer no procedure for holding bishops accountable, since current canon law makes no provision for sanctions against a bishop or cardinal who engages in acts of sexual abuse or its cover-up. Advocates have also argued that rather than waiting for the bishop and his diocesan review board to assess whether an abuse allegation merits sending to Rome for trial, all accused priests should be immediately removed from active ministry pending the completion of a full investigation. Further, in cases where church officials judge an accusation to be not credible or problematic and therefore not actionable, advocacy groups contend that victims should have a way to appeal such a decision.[17]

As mentioned above, there is also the crucial question of what, exactly, the canonical Essential Norms, as distinct from the Charter Promises, can address or require. Shortly after the release of the Norms in 2003, prominent theologian and respected canon lawyer Ladislas Orsy, SJ, offered a helpful analysis and evaluation that grapples with these precise questions. One of Orsy's conclusions reads,

> The *Norms* certainly provide some remedies for directly visible breakdowns. But the abuses went on for too long, and they spread too far to be just temporary and local problems; common sense tells us that there must be a deeper malaise in the social body of the Church. Its "immune system" was not working well for an extended time and in many places. An inquiry beyond the obvious is in order.[18]

In Orsy's judgment, then, the Norms may establish certain appropriate and reasonable policies. But neither the Charter nor the Norms were capable of fully addressing the underlying problems, the disease, in the life of the church that the sex abuse crisis had signaled.

In June 2004, the eminent Jesuit theologian Cardinal Avery Dulles offered perhaps the most critical assessment of the Charter and the Essential Norms. Without denying the bishops' obligations to address the grievous moral harm of young people and the communal scandal of the abuse crisis, Dulles argued that in adopting the Charter and Norms, the bishops had succumbed to societal pressure and, in the process, had strayed from long-held principles and values enshrined in Catholic doctrine, in canon law, and in some cases in civil law. In making his case, Dulles advanced fifteen principles, each of which, he argued, ought to be considered carefully during the two-year review of the Charter and Norms scheduled for later that year.[19] Among the issues Dulles lifted up for further attention are the following: the abandonment of a presumption of innocence; tendencies toward an overly broad or unclear definition of abuse; the jettisoning of the statute of limitations; failures to observe due process; and the wholesale vilification of the offending clergy with no attention to maintenance or recovery of the priestly identity for a priest no longer able to practice his office. Not surprisingly, Dulles's arguments received a mixed hearing among the bishops and wider church public. And notably, nowhere in his long list of concerns about the limitations of the Norms and Charter does Dulles raise the central question that Orsy poses: whether the fact of clergy abuse and the moral harm it has wrought indicate something so grievous about the state and condition of the church that a more probing analysis and diagnosis of the disease are required to understand it; and as a result, more extensive, thoroughgoing cultural and structural changes in the church will be needed to address it.

The Return of Crisis Management in the Summer of 2018

During the summer of 2018 two events occasioned new waves of anger and protest over clergy sexual abuse. The first major case was the public release of the Pennsylvania Grand Jury Report on July 27, 2018, which we investigated in the previous chapter. The second instance pertained to the accusations of sexual misconduct by Cardinal Theodore McCarrick, the retired cardinal archbishop of Washington, DC, which was the first public accusation against a cardinal. Rumors or testimonies about McCarrick's sexual abuse of seminarians, whether young adults or minors, had circulated among priests, bishops, and cardinals for years, maybe decades. At a minimum, Benedict XVI and Francis knew about these stories. A full investigation of the McCarrick case was initiated by the Vatican in October 2018, which led to McCarrick being put on trial and proven guilty of sexual misconduct with minors on January 11, 2019. On February 16, the Vatican announced that he had been laicized.

The Responses of Three Bishops of Rome

Pope John Paul II (1978–2005)

Shifting our attention from the local and national U.S. levels, let us step back and further consider the responses to this crisis by three popes. As we've seen, John Paul II advanced a conservative interpretation of the Second Vatican Council by implementing a policy of (re)centralization of authority in the pope and Vatican curia. Recall that the council had introduced decentralizing practices through its theological teaching about the bishops, which focused not just on individual bishops' work in their local church dioceses, but on the whole "college" of bishops, acting together in care for the universal church. Organizationally, Vatican II's teaching on the collegiality of bishops was advanced by the establishment of the synod of bishops—regular meetings of representative bishops from around the world, initiated by Pope Paul VI in the midst of the council—and by promoting the development of national and regional bishops' conferences.

John Paul II, who saw himself as a champion of Vatican II, was also an influential interpreter of the council and a primary arbiter of its implementation, especially through his roles in establishing the Revised Code of Canon Law (1983), in the formation and the release of the New Catechism of the Catholic Church (1992), and in developing and in many ways constraining the bishops' collegial discerning and teaching authority in synods and in national or episcopal conferences by placing restrictions on topics that could and could not be discussed. Moving away from the early post–Vatican II era, when every church policy seemed to be on the table for the college of bishops to weigh in on, Pope John Paul II banned open discussion on subjects that included the ordination of women and married men, birth control, and the use of condoms to prevent the spread of disease during the HIV-AIDS crisis. And as is well known, he was a staunch defender of strong pro-life stances on matters of abortion, euthanasia, and the death penalty.

This pope also played an important role in the evolving conceptions of the laity's participation and authority in the church during this period. In the council's immediate aftermath, between 1965 and 1985, there had been considerable development of lay ministries in the church. Laypeople took on important roles in liturgical ministries, in religious education, in charitable activities, and in work for justice. In keeping with Vatican II, John Paul II affirmed the identity and mission of the lay faithful people of God.[20] Yet by the mid-1980s, he began to give greater emphasis to the ontological and ministerial distinctiveness of the ordained clergy. Though these views were more associated with pre–Vatican II theologies, policies, and practices that understood priests as separate from and superior to the laity, under John Paul II's leadership they were reaffirmed and enforced at every level of the church.[21] Following the scandalous 1984 revelations about Gilbert Gauthe and their 1990s sequels concerning James Porter, Rudy Kos, and others, bishops and heads of religious orders began to petition Vatican curial offices to remove these men from priesthood. But they found John Paul II and the Vatican apparatus increasingly remote, nonresponsive, and slow to answer their requests.

As a champion of the distinctive and higher calling of priests, John Paul II promoted a theology of priesthood and seminary formation that conceded the shortcomings of much previous priestly formation and sought to advance a more holistic and integrated "Program for Priestly Formation."[22] In 2001,when many more accusations of clergy sexual abuse began to be reported, John Paul II added refinements to the canon laws pertaining to clerical sexual abuse of minors younger than eighteen.[23] The Congregation for the Doctrine of the Faith, with Cardinal Ratzinger as the prefect, was placed in charge of addressing the growing backlog of clergy sexual abuse cases. In 2002, when the *Boston Globe* began their series of reports, attention to clerical sex abuse by John Paul II and the Vatican further increased.

Here it's worth recalling the teachings of John Paul II on personal sin, social sin, and structural sin we discussed in chapter 2. As the new millennium approached, the pope began making a series of public apologies to individuals and groups who, in the past and present, had been harmed by the personal sins of members of the church. Remarkably, however, never once during this period of time did he apologize for clergy sexual abuse of minors or for the complicity of bishops in tolerating or covering up these actions. On April 22, 2002, during a meeting with the cardinals of the United States, the then eighty-two-year-old pope offered his most direct statement concerning the clerical sexual abuse of minors. Yet true to his view of sin, he did not speak of the sinfulness of the church, nor did he directly acknowledge the sinfulness of bishops. Rather, he blamed the excesses of the broader modern culture for priestly sexual immorality and the rise of homosexuality among priests. In the years that followed, his belief that homosexuality among priests was a factor in the sexual abuse of minors led John Paul to ban the admission to seminary of candidates with "deeply rooted homosexual tendencies."[24]

During the final years of his papacy, as the repercussions of the abuse scandal intensified in the United States and around the world, John Paul II's health continued to decline, and he was not active in addressing the crisis. In the end, his handling of the abuse crisis was one particular area in which this very popular pope received considerable criticism. Based on public evidence, he did not apologize in the name of the church, the bishops, or abusing priests either to the victims or to the members of the church who had their deep faith shaken to the core by the horrendous acts of their priests and bishops and by Vatican officials.[25] And if John Paul II ever met personally with abuse victims or their families, we have no public record of it.

In one particular case, the pope's limitations in addressing the abuse controversy became glaringly obvious. Mexican Father

Marcel Maciel Degollado was the founder of a powerful international religious congregation named the Legionaries of Christ. The charismatic Father Maciel, who had a reputation for inspiring great numbers of young men to enter his religious order, was also gifted at raising immense amounts of money for the Legionaries' ministries and donating a significant percentage of the funds he raised to the Vatican. In 1997, before the U.S. crisis came to full light, nine adult men accused Father Maciel of sexually abusing them as minors, in the 1940s and 1950s. But John Paul II, who counted Father Maciel as a friend and believed in his holiness, did not order a full investigation of these allegations, and no actions were taken against the Mexican priest.

After the pope died in 2005, a torrent of credible allegations against Maciel came to light. Besides abusing scores of young students and seminarians over the years, he was accused of having had relations with two women, one initially a minor. It was revealed that Maciel had fathered six children, two of whom he was also accused of sexually abusing. In 2006, in the wake of mounting evidence for the truth of these accusations, Pope Benedict XVI removed Maciel from his post as leader of the Legionaries of Christ and ordered him to spend the remainder of his life in seclusion, prayer, and penance.

Pope Benedict XVI (2005–2013)

Joseph Ratzinger, an influential theologian at Vatican II, was chosen by John Paul II to serve as prefect of the Congregation of the Doctrine of the Faith, a position he held from 1982 to 2005, when he was elected pope after his predecessor's death. As head of the CDF, Cardinal Ratzinger became a controversial figure, earning a reputation as a theological conservative. Over his twenty-four years in the office, he disciplined many progressive theologians who wrote and spoke out on contested issues in sexual ethics, liberation theology, and the theology of priesthood and the church.

With John Paul II, Cardinal Ratzinger defended the holiness of the church and the prominent status of ordained clergy. His theology of priesthood accentuated priests' unique character and authority and maintained that through ordination priests have special sacramental and governing powers in the church while circumscribing the roles to be played by the laity in the church governance and ministry. He was particularly critical of efforts to implement Vatican II by promoting open discussion and collective discernment between bishops and laypersons in episcopal conferences and synods.

As revelations of clergy sexual abuse escalated during the 1990s, there was increasing criticism of the slow and unreliable procedures by which curial officials were handling files on accused priests submitted to the Vatican for evaluation. In 2001, John Paul II appointed Ratzinger to take charge of evaluating cases of accused priests and making decisions about removing them from ministry, a change that earned Ratzinger credit for making the process more efficient and faster. Now the primary Vatican official in charge of making decisions about how to handle clergy abuse allegations, Ratzinger weekly evaluated many cases from around the world and especially from the United States.

When the Dallas Charter was released, however, Ratzinger was not inclined to support a policy of zero tolerance toward accused priest molesters, nor any requirement for their laicization. Instead, he pointed to the penal law of the church, which allowed suspension from priestly ministry but not laicization. And although he accelerated the process of evaluating accused priests, he neither spoke out nor took action against bishops for their mismanagement and complicity. Ratzinger was elected Pope Benedict XVI in 2005.

Addressing the U.S. Bishops during his 2008 papal visit, Pope Benedict echoed the opinion of Cardinal Francis George of Chicago, then the president of the USCCB, that the sexual abuse scandal "was very badly handled." Benedict also quoted from John Paul II's April 2002 speech to the U.S. Cardinals, hoping "that this time of trial will bring a purification of the entire Catholic community," which would contribute to "a holier priesthood, a holier episcopate, and a holier Church." Pope Benedict returned to these themes in his March 19, 2010, letter to the church in Ireland: "It cannot be denied that some of you [bishops] and your predecessors failed, at times grievously, to apply the long-established norms of canon law to the crime of child abuse. Serious mistakes were made in responding to allegations....It must be admitted that grave errors of judgment were made, and failures of leadership occurred. All of this seriously undermined your credibility."[26] The pope then turned to his often-repeated diagnosis of clergy sexual abuse of children as fomented by the societal context of secularization. In Benedict's eyes, secularization in Ireland had provided the determining context for "the disturbing problem of child sexual abuse" and its surrounding conditions, including the deterioration of priestly holiness and poor seminary formation, and "a tendency in [Irish] society to favor the clergy and other authority figures; and a misplaced concern for the reputation of the Church and the avoidance of scandal, resulting in failure to apply existing canonical penalties and to safeguard the dignity of every person."

As with his predecessor John Paul II, Benedict's views on sin, especially sin in the church, shaped what he was willing to say about the crisis. Throughout his years in Vatican leadership, his comments on accountability for clergy sexual abuse consistently emphasized the personal failures and sinfulness of priests, without acknowledging systemic or institutional sin in any form within the church as a whole or in its national or regional episcopal conferences or local churches. Whenever he addressed clergy sex abuse, he also spoke about a breakdown of civilization caused by modern currents of thought and societal secularization, which had impacted the area of sexual morality. These, according to Benedict, were the decisive contributing factors to the modern scandal of sexually abusive clergy.

He faults bishops for their failure of judgment in assessing the situations associated with clergy abuse, not for their personal moral failure nor for being involved in systemic structural failure in the church. In his address to the U.S. Bishops on April 16, 2008, he said it is insufficient to concentrate on changes in policies and programs: these need to be situated in "a wider context of degrading manifestations and the crude manipulation of sexuality so prevalent today."[27] This message was repeated throughout his trip in the United States in April 2008 and was emphasized in his March 19, 2010, letter to the church in Ireland, where he wrote, "You have suffered grievously, and I am truly sorry. I know that nothing can undo the wrong you have endured. Your trust has been betrayed and your dignity has been violated," which he attributed to the "sinful and criminal acts" of priests, which has caused the "grievous wound" that has been created in the church by "the secularization of Irish society."[28]

Let me conclude this overview of the responses to clergy sexual abuse across the Vatican career of Cardinal Joseph Ratzinger, later Pope Benedict, by looking at his treatment of the victims of clerical sexual abuse. Over his more than ten years at the CDF, Ratzinger spent immense amounts of time reviewing cases submitted by bishops, diocesan canon lawyers, and officials from around the world. Regularly, these reports described the horrific experiences undergone by those abused by priests, adducing these experiences as evidence in arguing for the laicization of priest-perpetrators. Yet only during his years as pope did he begin to visit with those who had suffered abuse. During Benedict's April 2008 papal visit to the United States, Cardinal Sean O'Malley, Bernard Law's replacement in Boston, arranged for the pope to meet with five Boston victims in Washington, DC. In media reports, those survivors described their moving encounters with the pope. Later, in his letter to the church in Ireland, Benedict wrote that "on several occasions since my election to the see of Peter, I have met with victims of sexual abuse, as indeed I am ready to do in the future. I have sat with them, I have listened to their stories, I have acknowledged their suffering, and I have prayed with them and for them." Similar meetings between Benedict and survivors took place in Australia, Malta, the United Kingdom, and Germany. It has also been reported that Benedict urged bishops to do likewise: meet with victims, listen to their stories, and pray with them.

On February 28, 2013, at the age of eighty-five, Benedict XVI became the first pope to resign since Gregory XII in 1415. There has been much speculation about why he chose to do so. According to one widely circulated opinion, during his final years in office Benedict became increasingly disheartened as he learned of the significant number of gay priests and cardinals at work in the Vatican and that some of the most outspoken Vatican critics of "homosexual" priests were themselves practicing homosexuals or intimate friends with gay clergy and gay cardinals in the hierarchy. These revelations were purportedly deeply discouraging to Benedict, who, as prefect of the CDF and then as pope, had crafted and defended the church's official moral repudiation of homosexuality and installed restrictions on admittance of seminarians with homosexual orientations or who participated in a gay "subculture."[29]

Another proximate factor in Benedict's resignation, many conjectured, was the financial problems associated with irregularities in the Vatican Bank. In the view of many, the strong resistance to reform at the Vatican Bank was not completely unrelated to the aforementioned issues surrounding clerics who surreptitiously lived lives contrary to their vows of celibacy. This financial institution had a history of being intertwined with the culture of secrecy and blackmail among clergy of the Vatican.

Did Ratzinger, who throughout his career held such a high theology of priesthood that emphasized the purity of the priest and the holiness of the church, find himself incapable of comprehending or effectively responding to these crises of church corruption? His own personal theology, which had largely become the official doctrine of the church, seemed to fall short in preventing or adequately dealing with clerical sexual abuse and Vatican corruption. Perhaps, in the words of Belgian theologian Lieven Boeve, Pope Benedict suffered from an acute experience of cognitive dissonance.[30] By the time of his resignation, his deepest and most cherished convictions about the church and priesthood were collapsing, and the weight of this reality may have been too much to bear any longer.[31] Is this, in fact, the case? We probably will never know.

Pope Francis (2013–)

Jorge Mario Bergoglio was elected pope on March 13, 2013, as the first Jesuit pope and the first from the Global South, born in Buenos Aires, Argentina. Too young to have attended Vatican II, as the previous five popes had done, Bergoglio traversed a rapid, dramatic, and at times contentious path to becoming an influential church leader.[32] Appointed bishop and later cardinal, over time he became an active and widely respected leader in the Diocese of Buenos Aires and in the Latin American Bishops Conference and played a key role in preparing the final document at their assembly in Aparecida in 2007.

From day one of his pontificate, the new Pope Francis had to exercise his office in the face of the worldwide scandal over clerical sexual abuse of minors. As we saw in chapter 2, Francis's understandings of personal, cultural, and institutional sin evolved over the course of his career. Especially after experiencing the institutional repercussions of his own authoritarian style of leadership as a young rector and provincial, and the social difficulties associated with the dirty war in Argentina and subsequent economic collapse, Francis began to speak and write about the role of personal sin in contributing to institutional and systemic corruption. In grappling with the crisis of clergy sex abuse, Pope Francis has further developed this argument about sin and systemic corruption, especially in his analysis of the failures of bishops at the diocesan and curial levels of the church.

In July 2014, thirteen months after being elected pope, Francis met for the first time with victims of clergy sexual abuse in the Vatican and begged for their forgiveness for the sexual abuse itself and for the failures of the church to respond appropriately to their accusations.[33] A second meeting took place in Philadelphia in September 2015 between Francis and five abuse survivors.[34] On February 15, 2018, it was reported that the pope has since met almost weekly with survivors, to listen to their stories, to pray with them, and to ask for their forgiveness for the church's role in the evil and suffering they have undergone.[35]

As was mentioned in chapter 2, Francis's outreach to abuse survivors has not been without flaws and mistakes. One glaring example is associated with the disastrous meetings between Francis, survivors, and a deeply wounded Chilean church during his January 15–18, 2018, papal visit. Francis's Chilean journey was intended to provide an opportunity to reach out to survivors and to promote reconciliation and healing in the church in the aftermath of devastating revelations of clergy sexual abuse in this largely Catholic country. Instead of healing, however, Francis offended Chilean Catholics when he accused three respected abuse survivors of slandering Bishop Juan Barros, a person Francis had mentored and appointed bishop in 2015, for claiming that Barros had covered up the sex abuse of minors by a notorious predator priest. The resulting uproar caused a major controversy for Francis and threatened to jeopardize all the work he was doing to address clergy sex abuse.

Francis then took a number of steps to more fully investigate and transparently address the Chilean sex abuse crisis. First, he sent two trusted Vatican officials, Archbishop Charles Scicluna and Monsignor Jordi Bertomeu, to New York and Chile to interview survivors and witnesses and to report back on their findings. Second, on April 8, 2018, he invited all the bishops of Chile (thirty-four, including auxiliary bishops) to come to Rome for meetings May 15–17 to discern the matter with him. Third, on April 28–29 he met personally with several Chilean victims of abuse to seek to make amends.[36] Next, when Francis met with all the bishops of Chile in mid-May, he asked for their resignations for their complicity and corruption. All submitted written resignations, and seven resignations were immediately approved by the pope, with the possibility of more to come. Finally, after meeting with the bishops, Francis sent a letter of apology for his own errors and faults on May 31 to "the Pilgrim People of God in Chile," which I will comment on further below.[37]

As was described in the last chapter, two other events during the summer of 2018 occasioned new waves of anger and protest over clergy sexual abuse. The first was the public release of the Pennsylvania Grand Jury Report on July 27, 2018. The second was the *New York Times* report of July 16, 2018, on the sexual misconduct of the retired Cardinal Theodore McCarrick, the first public accusation of abuse to be leveled against a cardinal.[38] After a Vatican investigation and a trial in October 2018, McCarrick was found guilty and subsequently laicized.

These dramatic events, especially the grand jury report, received widespread attention in the press and seemed to reopen the wounds of abuse in the U.S. church once again, regardless of the fact that most of the incidents had occurred years or even decades earlier. As a result, the U.S. Bishops felt obliged to address this issue at their next semiannual meeting in November 2018. Recall that one of the key issues left unaddressed in the Dallas Charter was how to assess and process allegations of sex abuse or its cover-up by bishops, archbishops, or cardinals at the provincial or national level. In advance of the November meeting, organizers devised a plan whereby the U.S. Bishops in attendance would discern and decide on a course of action to be taken in cases of bishops, archbishops, or cardinals found to have sexually abused minors or to have been involved in the cover-up of abuse in their dioceses. A bishops' organizing committee crafted an innovative new procedure for discussion and voting on this matter at the November meeting; but before the November USCCB meeting was to begin, the president of the conference received orders from the Vatican that the assembled U.S. Bishops were not to take any votes on this issue.

The Vatican's directive to the U.S. Bishops not to vote on this matter, without any accompanying explanation, confused many Catholics and prompted others to suspect that the pope was foot-dragging on this issue. Only months later, during an airplane interview on May 31, 2019, did Francis shed light on his reasons. As reported by Joshua McElwee,

> Francis said the proposals, which included the creation of a new commission including laypeople to review allegations of abuse made against bishops, were "too much" like those that could be expected from a nonprofit organization and "neglected" the spiritual dimension of fighting the evil of sexual abuse. "The church is not a Congregationalist church," said Francis. "It is a Catholic Church, where the bishop must take on the responsibility, like a pastor." This line of argument appears in his January 2019 letter to the U.S. bishops: the bishops' credibility would not be regained by "simply creating new committees or improving flow charts."[39]

Pope Francis would invoke this argument again as the year went on to discourage dramatic structural change and, in particular, to decline to support lay involvement in the oversight of bishops and clergy and in decision-making capacities in diocesan leadership and processes to ensure the church's accountability and responsibility. Francis confirmed that accusations against a cardinal, an archbishop, or a bishop could not be initiated by a board led by laypeople; canonically, these actions were reserved to the pope and curial offices. In the United States, some bishops were relieved to take the USCCB's proposal, which had been developed in a rather short amount of time, off the table. But this meant that the unresolved issues that the USCCB proposal had been intended to address were left unaddressed and unresolved. These issues would receive further discussion in February 2019 when the presidents of episcopal conferences throughout the world met in Rome.

By the end of 2018, a great limitation of the 2002 Dallas Charter and Norms had taken center stage: neither the Charter nor the Norms provided protocols for holding bishops and cardinals accountable for their own sexual abuse of minors or their abuses of power in handling cases of clergy abuse. Many people, regardless of religious beliefs, were paying attention to this news, and they were increasingly outraged.[40]

Francis Convenes a Summit in 2019

On September 12, 2018, Vatican officials announced an innovative gathering of bishops from around the world to take place February 21–24, 2019. The presidents of all national and regional episcopal conferences were being convened to address the underlying issues involved in the sex abuse crisis. The much-anticipated gathering came to be called the Protection of Minors in the Church: Responsibility, Accountability, Transparency.

Francis advised the presidents of episcopal conferences to prepare for this Vatican meeting by spending time with victim-survivors in their own dioceses and regions. At each session of the February assembly in Rome, the bishops first heard short testimonies from victim-survivors. These were followed by a thirty-minute address by a cardinal or bishop, after which bishops gathered for small group discussions. The three-day gathering ended with an address by Pope Francis.[41]

What Francis said (and did not say) in his culminating address left certain U.S. Catholic advocacy groups quite dissatisfied.[42] They had hoped he would issue new policies mandating stricter approaches to zero tolerance and to punishing offending clergy and bishops for every diocese in the global church. But issuing such universal rules ran contrary to Francis's efforts to decentralize decision-making in the church and to support bishops' own collegial and synodal authority. In this vein, some bishops from Africa and Asia who had initially stated that they viewed clerical sexual abuse of minors to be a solely U.S. and European problem were moved to change their perspectives by the victims' testimonies offered at the February Vatican meeting. Soon thereafter, reports that drew public attention to the sexual abuse of women religious in the Global South as well as in the North underscored the fact that clerical abuse was a problem that no diocese or region could simply deny or ignore.

Awareness of this complex mixture of global concerns and attitudes had, in fact, shaped the agenda of the entire February meeting as well as the tenor of Pope Francis's closing remarks. Even granting this, it was undeniable to all those present as well as to public observers that the February gathering had failed to address the glaring gap in the Dallas Charter that was now becoming the standard used by bishops around the world: there remained no straightforward procedure for holding bishops and cardinals accountable either for their own acts of sex abuse, or for their mismanagement, corruption, and cover-ups in handled offenses of their priests.

In fact, one potentially promising approach to this unaddressed issue had surfaced in the run-up to the U.S. Bishops' November 2018 meeting, but, due to the Vatican's intervention, it was not brought to a vote. By church law, episcopal conferences do not have the authority to assess and judge the sexual behavior and the administrative mismanagement of bishops and cardinals.

Only Vatican officials can. This means that when a bishop or cardinal is suspected or accused of wrongdoing, fellow bishops and cardinals in their national church, with no authority to judge those of equal rank, also lack any procedures for conducting an inquiry that would entail gathering evidence and evaluating the accusation's credibility.

To redress this, the U.S. Bishops had proposed drawing upon a long-standing hierarchical structure and enlisting the services in such cases of a metropolitan archbishop. A metropolitan is a bishop from a major city in a geographical region, called an ecclesiastical province, who is appointed by the Vatican to serve that province. The metropolitan's duties include promoting communication and deliberation among a select group of regional bishops, called suffragan bishops, who work with the metropolitan archbishop to promote the good of the church in their province.[43]

In the spring following the pope's February 2019 gathering with the presidents of episcopal conferences, Pope Francis made two major policy decisions. First, he took a decisive step forward on his own initiative by issuing *Vos Estis Lux Mundi* on May 7, 2019. This document approved the metropolitan solution initially introduced by the U.S. Bishops, interpreting canons 435–36 to allow metropolitans to evaluate with a committee accusations brought against a bishop or a cardinal of personal involvement in the sexual abuse of minors, here extended to age eighteen, or of taking courses of action or omission that obstruct or evade "civil or canonical investigations, whether administrative or penal" against a clergy person who was found to be engaged in sinful and criminal behavior.[44] In instances when this investigative committee reaches a conclusion, by voting, that the case against a cardinal or bishop is justified, their conclusion was to be submitted to the appropriate Vatican office for further consideration.

Significantly, the document allowed, but did not require, the involvement of qualified laypeople in the metropolitan review process. Because Francis issued no requirement that laypeople be involved in processes of reviews and structures of accountability, *Vos Estis Lux Mundi* was susceptible to the criticism that once again this model left only fellow clerics (bishops) holding bishops accountable.[45] We are left, then, with an important question: What other options or avenues are available for supplementing and further strengthening what Francis has established thus far and made possible? We will explore this question in the next chapter.

There was a second major policy consequence of the meeting of presidents of episcopal conferences. At the end of 2019 Pope Francis revoked and abolished the long-standing policy of papal secrecy in cases involving the sexual misconduct of clergy, including bishops and cardinals, and their concealment of clerical abuse. This change, which was widely welcomed, was also widely viewed as long overdue.

Conclusion

In reply to the widespread criticisms of the responses to clergy sex abuse by individual bishops, the U.S. episcopal conference, and the last three popes, this chapter has offered an overview of the most noteworthy courses of action taken by the body of U.S. Bishops and the popes. These plots in the larger narrative exhibit church leaders' learning curve, their achievements, and their limitations. Yet a larger purpose is at work here. Besides offering a reckoning of important courses of action, this chapter has tried to clarify selected undercurrents at work in the operation of church authority and decision-making, the tectonic shift from a more centralized to a more decentralized approach in church governance and by so doing to surface issues not yet sufficiently discussed and addressed.

Previous chapters have recounted stories of individual bishops who behaved disgracefully and discredited their office and the church. Their actions illustrate graphically the harm perpetrated by individual leaders' sins and wrongdoings. When the U.S. Bishops' Conference in 1985 failed to seriously engage the document that was prepared for them, "The Problem of Sexual Molestation by Roman Catholic Clergy," their failure indicated deeper cultural patterns and institutional policies that had fostered secrecy, complicity, and concealment. Yet, the bishops' two-day workshop Think

Tank on clergy abuse in 1993; their preparation and dissemination of a two-volume manual, *Restoring Trust*, in 1994; and the 2002 Dallas Charter and Norms, did represent incremental achievements on the part of the U.S. Episcopal Conference. Too often, along the way, individual bishops were slow learners, laggards, and resistant to these learnings. Acknowledging this, and without denying the flaws and limitations of the efforts of the body of U.S. Bishops, it is possible to detect herein some good-faith efforts that continued to be constrained by corrupt cultures and systemic problems.

The early decades of the clergy abuse public scandal, which took place in the 1980s and 1990s during the papacies of John Paul II and Benedict XVI, brought to light previous decades of covert clergy abuse and episcopal malfeasance going back to the 1950s. John Paul II, for all his strengths and genuine accomplishments, fostered a highly centralized vision of the church that contributed to a notoriously deficient approach to facing cases of clergy sexual abuse. Benedict XVI largely shared his predecessor's centralized ecclesial vision, yet he came more fully to realize and to address publicly the personal corruption of priests. But Benedict tended to blame modern secular culture and progressive movements in theology as the main incentives for these problems, and he failed to offer a sufficiently deep analysis of the cultural and institutional character of sin and systemic corruption within the church and its role in breeding and tolerating the scandal of clergy sexual abuse.

The failures of these two popes to recognize and sufficiently analyze the cultural and systemic issues within the church that were contributing to these problems were intertwined with their centralized, pyramidal vision of the church. In the wake of Ratzinger's first-hand exposure to the number of accused priests and his personal encounters with victim-survivors after becoming pope, he recognized more clearly the magnitude of the problems involved but never provided the necessary theological and organizational vision to address them. As a result, the deeper causes of the problems involved, including the dysfunctions of clericalism and hierarchicalism, were never adequately named.

The papacy of Francis initiated a new phase in the reception of the documents of Vatican II, especially its teaching on the bishop's office and on episcopal collegiality. This shift became especially evident in Francis's promotion of a "sound decentralization" of policies and practices, and his heralding of a polycentric vision of the universal church—imaged as a polyhedron not a sphere—that promoted listening to and learning from the distinctive voices and contributions from peoples of the Global South, the peripheries, and the marginalized. These are major accomplishments. Francis has also fostered and modeled greater sensitivity and receptiveness to the views of national and regional bishops' conferences around the world, especially in the Global South, and he has been an outspoken defender of an open and honest discussion of taboo subjects during bishops' triennial synods. These policies have facilitated far greater attention to the problems of clericalism and hierarchicalism in the church and more open advocacy of transparency, accountability, and responsibility among bishops. Francis's particular vision of the roles of bishops, the synod of bishops, and episcopal conferences has also been at the forefront of his approach to clergy sex abuse and episcopal malfeasance.

In my own judgment, for all its strengths and appeal, Francis's program also has limitations. Francis is rightly recognized for the attention he has given to the vision of the church as the whole faithful people of God. And he has emphasized the importance of bishops and priests not only accompanying, but also listening and being responsive to, the sense of all the faithful in their communities, including laypeople, women, and especially the poor and the marginalized. Yet, as we have seen, Pope Francis has been of two minds when it comes to the laity. In his vision, the ordained, bishops and priests, should listen to the laity in collective processes of synodal discernment. However, the laity should not be given decision-making authority when it comes to councils and synods and review boards evaluating cases of clergy sex abuse and especially in cases of episcopal corruption and complicity. Only bishops can decide in matters of substance, leaving laypeople perhaps with some voice, but with neither a vote nor genuine authority when it comes to any level of official decision-making in the church. When laypeople have called for such authority Francis has dismissed their laments and aspirations as failing to distinguish between spiritual discernment and calls for changes in decision-making structures that would remake the church into something more like a nongovernmental organization (NGO) or a congregationalist denomination or a parliamentary procedure. In Francis's frequently used imagery, the priests and bishops are the shepherds leading the pilgrimage and the flock, the laypeople are the sheep.

This pope has a track record of welcoming open debate and even conflict in the church and in civil society as opportunities for people to move beyond polarities and dialectics and to find new avenues for the daughters and sons of God to freely welcome and realize their callings. While acknowledging the advancements made by Francis's policies, their limitations suggest that we must take his advice by pressing on in open debate and contestation over these far-from-resolved matters. Specifically, members of the church need to engage in renewed efforts of our productive imaginations in order to conceive of and cultivate a new ecclesial social and cultural imaginary that affirms the roles of the ordained, bishops and priests, but accords more substantive authority to laypeople. This vexed issue is at the heart of contemporary efforts to realize synodality at every level of the church. It is, as well, at the crux of long-standing problems and causes that have contributed to the underlying issues involved in the scandal of clergy sex abuse. The next chapter will explore these underlying issues.

Chapter 5

Changes Long Resisted

Up to this point, we have observed a number of different proposals for addressing clergy sexual abuse of minors and bishops' mismanagement of these crimes. Victim-survivors, their allies, media witnesses, and legal advocates have called on both civil authorities and church officials to undertake legal processes and punitive measures against those responsible, and they have appealed for ongoing care and reparations for those who have been harmed. These proposals have wide support among U.S. Catholics, even Catholics who are rankled by the vitriol of the public discourse that prophetic voices have at times evoked.

As we have also seen, U.S. bishops and the last three popes have developed their own responses to address the scandal of clergy abuse of minors. Many Catholics, including those who have found it difficult or impossible to remain involved in the church, regard the kinds of response developed by the U.S. bishops and Pope Francis as rightly called for and long overdue. Yet for many other active and former Catholics, including those who are receptive to Francis's vision of the church and his efforts to address the scandal, programmatic changes in policies and practices do not go far enough. On their own they cannot begin to address the deeper and central cultural, structural, and systemic problems and destructive exercises of church power that lie at the roots of these crises.

In this chapter I invite readers to imagine what changes you would propose that could help address the causes that have contributed to the clergy sex abuse of minors and the dysfunctions in the church this crisis reveals, going beyond the remedies we have already explored. This invitation to you, the reader, to engage your own productive imagination in seeking ways to address the wounds and dysfunctions of the church, returns us to the core question of this book: How might the sexual abuse scandal help generate new, more fruitful ways of thinking and acting within the church in controversy?

To encourage your own reflections, I will introduce several avenues of response to the crisis that have not been introduced in the previous chapters. None of these proposals are entirely new; various sectors in the church have raised each of them, especially in the aftermath of Vatican II. All of them have resurfaced and are being discussed more widely in this context.

Fully Recognizing the Equality and Authority of All the Baptized

A first avenue of response focuses on fully recognizing the equality and authority of all baptized members of the church. Clergy sex abuse of minors combined with the malfeasance of bishops not only violates moral codes and the codes of civil justice in many countries around the world, but it also desecrates baptized believers. As we have seen, Vatican II developed pivotal teachings about the equality and giftedness of all baptized Christians, as the foundation of their participation in what have traditionally been called the priestly, prophetic, and kingly offices of Jesus Christ. This set of convictions, grounded in scriptural testimonies, laid the groundwork for a more robust theology and praxis of reciprocity and collaboration among all the faithful in the life of the church; in particular, this entailed collaboration of the laity with ordained priests and bishops in the church's ministries and mission. After the council, new forms of this collaboration began to be implemented in many, but not in all local parishes and dioceses. However, they have never been consistently promoted, advanced, or maintained. The promise of the council in this regard has often been undermined, if not rejected.

As we have also seen, the years after the council were challenging ones, combining pastoral experimentation with frustration. The core teachings of Vatican II about the equal baptismal dignity and active participation of the laity were affirmed in principle in postconciliar teachings and in the revised code of canon law issued in 1983. But during the papacies of John Paul II and Benedict XVI, Vatican II's teachings on the equality and newly recognized authority of all the baptized were undermined, as new restrictions were placed on the exercise of lay leadership and ministries, and hierarchal and clerical power and authority were accentuated and reasserted. Theologically, these changes reinforced an asymmetrical approach to the holiness and power of priests and bishops relative to the laity. At the grassroots level, laypeople, including women religious, have usually not been recognized as equal partners with priests and bishops in communal discernment and decision-making about ministry and mission.

Clergy sexual abuse combined with episcopal concealment and malfeasance both reflected and compounded restrictive—and frequently destructive—power dynamics that have drowned out the voices of the lay faithful and suppressed their free and honest participation in the communicative action within their church communities that is their baptismal calling and right. Studies of the dysfunctional communication and actions surrounding clergy sexual abuse of minors in the Catholic Church have regularly found connections with patterns of clerical authoritarianism and in-group protection within an all-male celibate clergy, which priest offenders often combined with manifestations of narcissism and an absence of empathy. Scholars like Keenan and Frawley-O'Dea have perceived in these traits a form of hypermasculinity, operating as a strong vision of patriarchy that promotes an infantilized view of the laity and at times misogyny, which harbors a defensive contempt of women, particularly of women with leadership skills and well-founded convictions. Of course, we can assume that there are some clergy, including bishops and cardinals, who do not have these personality traits and tendencies, but determining the percentages would require further study. To the extent that priest-hood attracts or fosters a culture supportive of men who exhibit an authoritarian personality, whether aggressive or demure in style, there is reason for concern about the openness of these ordained leaders to recognize the laity's baptismal equality, or to enter into genuine partnership with laypersons in the exercise of authority and decision-making in Catholic Church communities.

What have been the results of this trend to recentralize and reassert clerical primacy and authority? To point to only one of many disheartening outcomes: Gifted lay faithful are restrained from preaching in the context of eucharistic assemblies, regardless of their spiritual wisdom, personal skills, and training. As a result, communities of faith cannot benefit from the God-given charisms of those who are members of their community. Here we will focus attention on another outcome: the fact that the laity have regularly been denied the ability to cultivate and utilize their leadership abil-ities, in particular by exercising power in collective discernment and decision-making in the church. The voice of the lay faithful and the weight of their authority in matters of decision-making on matters of pastoral ministry, mission priorities for the local church, and participatory structures of responsibility and accountability have been consistently reduced to "consultative" only.

This imbalance is structurally inscribed in canon law (CIC), and in policies that do not require active discernment and decision-making roles for laypeople (CIC §129); for example, establishing parish pastoral councils is an optional prerogative of the bishop to decide after hearing the presbyteral council (§536); likewise, diocesan pastoral councils can be formed "to the extent that pas-toral circumstances suggest it" (§511). In 2002, when the USCCB approved the Charter for the Protection of Children and Young People, the corresponding Essential Norms called for each dio-cese to form a review board, as "a confidential consultative body" to assess accusations against priests. But in a 2019 investigation of numerous review boards across the United States, the Associ-ated Press reported that mandatory review boards "appointed by bishops and operating in secrecy have routinely undermined sex abuse claims from victims, shielded accused priests and helped the church avoid payouts."[1] Whatever the motivation or accuracy of this investigation, and however anecdotal its findings might be and how far they might fall short of scientific standards, this report draws attention to two crucial facts that are beyond reproach: while these review boards do include laypersons, and often professionals such as lawyers, members are chosen by the bishop, and the board's role is limited to consultation. Members advise the bishop, and the bishop then reaches his own decision.

As detailed in the last chapter, in *Vos Estis Lux Mundi*, Pope Francis established a particular metropolitan version of a review board, although not called a review board but identified by its task to investigate and determine whether the accusations made against a bishop or a cardinal merit submitting the case to the appropriate Vatican office. To make its judgment, a metropolitan convenes and leads a review board that may, but need not, include lay members and does not require that members take a vote on the merits of the accusation. Here again, institutionalized constraints appear to call into question the equality and authority of baptized lay members in the church.

We also should not lose sight of the fact that the diseases of clericalism and hierarchicalism, implicated in many of the harms inflicted on laypersons in the church, have also inflicted harm on priests themselves. These diseases and dysfunctions infiltrate seminary formation programs, institutional structures, policies that determine job placements, and diocesan cultures where they breed conditions for priests' overwork, overextension, isolation, and loneliness. Priests also experience the effects of these interconnected diseases when their own baptismal equality, voice, and viewpoints are disregarded in their relationships with bishops or religious superiors.

The clericalism and hierarchicalism that infect the body of the church damage all the baptized, lay and ordained alike. These pernicious viruses have bred the conditions for, and contributed to, the harms that abusive clergy have inflicted on children and the vulnerable, and on their wider circles of family, friends, and communities. The wounds of clergy abuse cannot be healed without first confronting their multiple symptoms, and then addressing their deeper causes. Ultimately, complete healing will occur only in the fullness of time, when all the forms of accountability and responsibility are disclosed, and divine justice and mercy are meted out.

More broadly, the diseases of clericalism and hierarchicalism are also implicated in restrictions placed on the lay baptized that cripple their ability to freely engage in open and honest communication on matters of conflict and controversy in the church. One need not deny the role of priestly and episcopal ordination and office in the life of the church, and the importance of the scholarly expertise of theologians in handing on the living tradition of the church and participating in the formulation of doctrine and reform in the church. However, priests, bishops, and theologians cannot fulfill their offices and roles unless they actively acknowledge and encourage all the faithful's important charisms and summons to play their parts as guardians of memory and as attuned to the voice of the Spirit in the sense of the faithful and the laments of those suffering injustice. Engaging in the collaboration of laypersons and ordained individuals provides lessons and shapes patterns of behavior that are essential to the proper formation of priests and bishops, and evidence of commitment to such partnerships should be a key criterion for their selection for ordination. And if this is the case, by logical extension, the faithful should be actively involved in the final processes leading to ordination and in the selection of bishops.

I have described how the equality and authority of the baptized are espoused, defended, and advanced in the teachings of the Second Vatican Council, but I have also emphasized how the laity's exercise of that equality and authority have been weakened and restricted in the council's aftermath. These developments reflect one dominant trajectory and story line in the history of the reception of the council's teaching on these matters. But this history also begs larger questions concerning others whose equality, authority, voices, and stances have been ignored, unrecognized, and denied in the church, as well as in civil society. These questions bring our attention back to marginalized and peripheral voices in the church, the voices of the poor, of peoples of color, and of immigrant populations and other vulnerable groups who have suffered as a result of clerical abuse and episcopal malfeasance. When we pose these questions in the twenty-first-century U.S. church, we cannot help but be shamed by the long history of Catholics' culpable ignorance and prejudice against the victims of settler colonialism among Native American Indians, and the victims of colonialism and slavery among African Americans, people from Latin America and the Caribbean, and many other Asian immigrant communities. This history has had countless ill effects, including on the ways vulnerable families and communities have been targeted and harmed by abusive clergy.

Clergy sex abuse of minors could be viewed as on a continuum with other forms of sexual, racial, and gender violence advanced by Catholics, often under the guise of an allegedly pure vision of clerical sanctity and hierarchical order, paired with perverse assumptions about purportedly "natural" ethnic and racial superiorities. As we confront the endless history of racism in U.S. society, we must raise equally difficult questions about how these interrelated dynamics and dysfunctions operate in cases of clergy sex abuse.

Reconsidering Priesthood

Since the actions of ordained men have been the source of this controversy, it seems fitting to consider proposals for reforms of the priesthood, many of which have also long been avoided and resisted. Calls for the reform of priesthood over the last twenty or thirty years in response to the clergy sex abuse scandal must be situated in the context of earlier calls for the reform of priesthood reaching back to the mid-twentieth century. Here I will comment only on reforms that explicitly speak to the abuse crisis.

Three changes will be considered here: (1) ending the mandatory celibacy requirement for priesthood; (2) initiating a synodal process to discern and deliberate over ordaining women to priesthood; and (3) lifting the ban on admitting candidates for entrance into the seminary due to their sexual orientation. Imagine the Roman Catholic Church with celibate male priests working alongside ordained celibate women and married men and women, both gay and straight. These changes, which would require in certain instances doctrinal developments as well as reforms of policies and practice, would mark a turning point in the church. But as important as they would be, would they resolve the factors that led to the sexual abuse crisis?

To preview what I will argue, I believe these changes would only represent a genuine turning point, a real conversion of the church, if they represented not only a remedy for the abuse crisis, but a shift to genuinely synodal processes of discernment and decision-making that include the active participation of representatives of the lay faithful in all deliberations. Importantly, these changes could only occur if the church's teaching on sexuality and gender evolve, doctrinally and practically.

Rescinding Mandatory Celibacy for Priestly Ordination?

Is celibacy the cause of clergy sex abuse? There is no empirical and statistical data to prove that it is. Could it be a significant factor among others? There are many scholars, including psychologists and sociologists, who believe that it cannot be ruled out as an important factor.[2] If the pope and bishops chose to establish an option for the clergy to marry, this could be a positive catalyst, perhaps even an important one, in addressing the systemic cultural issues that contributed to clergy sex abuse of minors and adults, but it would not be the decisive factor.

There are, after all, married clergy in other Christian traditions and communities, as well as many married male teachers, coaches, and counselors who have been accused and convicted of sexual abuse of minors. It is also true that large numbers of priests are able to live out the best qualities of celibate life in a grace-filled way. Without regarding it as a cure, then, we can consider whether dismantling mandatory celibacy as currently practiced might contribute to lessening destructive clericalism overall and thus, indirectly, to address the abuse crisis.

Clerical celibacy is not, as Roman Catholic Church tradition attests, a divinely ordained mandate. For roughly the first millennium, male leaders in the Christian community, who came to be identified as priests, deacons, and bishops, were allowed to marry, even though the virtues of chastity and celibacy were recognized and even encouraged by St. Paul and in the Gospels as valuable ways to witness to and advance the kingdom of God proclaimed by Jesus. The question whether to *require* celibacy in Western Christianity has been addressed at various church councils, notably at the Second Lateran Council (1139) and at the Council of Trent (1548–68), but this need not mean the question has been closed.

The question of permitting married clergy, formulated as "optional celibacy," began to receive renewed attention and increased discussion beginning in 1959 during preparations for the Second Vatican Council (1962–65).[3] Pope John XXIII acknowledged that celibacy was not an immutable teaching or law, but a church discipline that could change. He was not inclined to pursue it, however, since he expected it would be intensely debated during the council. But this discussion did not occur at the council, either before or after John's death in 1963. Paul VI, his successor, wrote to the council bishops that "it is not opportune to discuss this topic in public because it requires great prudence and is of great importance."[4] Among some bishops involved in the council and many other ordained and nonordained Catholics, Pope Paul's restriction was met with a measure of disappointment and anger.

Paul VI sought to bring to closure discussion of optional married priests in a 1967 encyclical. At the 1971 synod of bishops on ministerial priesthood the topic was again raised, but because many other issues took precedence it was not pursued.[5] Twenty years later John Paul II issued an apostolic exhortation on the Formation of Priests, which reflected the results of the 1990 synod of bishops on this topic.[6] This document is widely credited with advancing a holistic and integrated reform of priestly formation in seminaries. But it also staunchly defended mandatory celibacy. In the words of John Paul II, "The synod does not wish to leave any doubts in the mind of anyone regarding the Church's firm will to maintain the law that demands perpetual and freely chosen celibacy for present and future candidates for priestly ordination in the Latin rite."[7]

The requirement of mandatory celibacy for Latin-Rite Catholic priests does not pertain to Eastern-Rite Catholics, who ordain both married and unmarried priests, and it does not apply to Protestant ordained ministers (including Anglican priests). Amid controversies in the Anglican Communion about ordaining women as priests and bishops, blessing same-sex marriages, and ordaining gays and lesbians, the Vatican began to receive requests from married Anglican/Episcopalian priests who wished to become priests in the Roman Catholic tradition. In 1980 John Paul II approved this course of action, so that Roman Catholic bishops who wished to could receive these men, many of whom were married, as Catholic priests in their dioceses. This step has been both controversial and ambiguous, raising a number of questions about the true importance of mandatory celibacy in the Roman Catholic Church. Why, for example, was the ordination of celibate women in the Episcopal Church so offensive as to be judged as a valid reason to permit married men to function in the Catholic Church? And if these married men could become Roman Catholic priests, why could not married men who were born and raised as Catholics become ordained?

Pope Francis has contributed another variable to this ongoing discussion. Before he was elected pope, Francis espoused a position close to the stance of John XXIII. In a conversation with a rabbi in 2010 in Buenos Aires he observed that celibacy "is a matter of discipline, not of faith.[8] It can change." But he added that "for the moment, I am in favor of maintaining celibacy, with all its pros and cons, because we have ten centuries of good experiences rather than failures....Tradition has weight and authority."[9] But don't the clergy sex abuse of minors, as well as the sexual abuse of women religious and laywomen, including in concubinage, secret marriage, and other forms of illicit partnerships, together offer more than sufficient evidence regarding mandatory celibacy's "cons?" Do they tip the scales in support of allowing optional married clergy?

As pope, Francis seems to have little interest in opening this question of optional married clergy for discussion in the universal church. However, he has on several occasions expressed openness to considering ordaining married men with proven virtue (*vir probati*), if bishops' conferences were to ask that such an idea be considered under conditions of pressing need. Francis has encouraged bishops to explore this idea in their episcopal conferences and national bishops' councils;[10] and in October 2019, the policy of ordaining proven men was formally endorsed at the Pan-Amazon Region Synod of Bishops by a vote of 128 to 41.[11]

While he presumably expected this outcome, Pope Francis appeared unsettled by it, perhaps because there was not a peaceful consensus at the end of this vote, which in his eyes would have signified the Spirit at work. Whether this was the pope's rationale or not, instead of ratifying the position of the more than two-thirds majority, Francis decided not to pursue the ordination of married men in the region, at least not now.[12] As he later explained, there was "an atmosphere that ends up distorting, reducing and dividing the synod hall into dialectical and antagonistic positions that in no way help the mission of the church." Francis acknowledged that "there was a discussion...a rich discussion...a well-founded discussion, but no discernment, which is something different from arriving at a good and justified consensus or relative majority." Based on this synodal experience, he explains that "we must understand that the Synod is more than a parliament; and in this specific case it could not escape this dynamic. On this subject it has been a rich, productive, even necessary parliament; but no more than that. For me this was decisive in the final discernment." Francis's written remarks conclude, "I like to think that, in a certain sense, the Synod is not finished. This time of welcoming the whole process that we have lived through challenges us to continue to walk together and to put this experience into practice."[13]

Had he decided to ordain married men, it would, no doubt, have provided a precedent, which other regional synods or episcopal conferences in the Global South could then follow. Leading bishops from episcopal conferences in the Global North, such as Germany, have also stated their interest in pursuing such a course of action in their own countries. But for the time being, Francis chose not to pursue this option.

To be clear, the notion of ordaining *vir probati* is distinct from "optional celibacy." Rather than allowing young men who are studying for priesthood to marry, the proposal discussed at the Amazon Synod, instead, is to ordain to priesthood some married men who are now permanent deacons, under certain conditions and with restrictions. In addition, as voted upon by the Amazon Synod participants, the proposal only pertained to the exercise of sacramental ministries. No process of priestly formation for their teaching and governing roles was discussed.

What we've seen so far suggests that the issue of celibacy concerns more than just the question of whether or not a priest refrains from sexual relations. It raises a number of further, complicated questions. If married priests were allowed, what kinds of married men will and will not be accepted for ordination by the existing Catholic hierarchy? Keep in mind that under recent papacies, respected priests who support, or at least are not against considering, optional celibacy generally were not chosen to be bishops. At the same time, recent revelations about clerical sexual abuse of both minors and adult women and men have also revealed that even at times when traditionalist bishops have predominated, the church has often maintained a kind of don't-ask-don't-tell stance on clerical sexual activity. Ironically, the best case for officially allowing clergy to minister publicly while also living sacramental vows of marriage may be the increasing evidence that many priests and bishops are already practicing "optional celibacy," in the dark and without protections for their partners.

But would allowing married priests to perform the sacraments, or to teach and govern, really help alleviate the sources of abuse? Only, I would say, if the equality, voices, and authority of the lay baptized are simultaneously more fully engaged and honored, rather than ignored, constricted, or undermined by ordained men, whether married or celibate.

Ordaining Women to Priesthood?

It is noteworthy that the "circumstances of the present day" addressed by John Paul II in his 1992 document on priestly formation, *Pastores Dabo Vobis*, did not include one word about clergy sex abuse of minors, even though this had been on the radar of Roman curial offices at least since the 1980s in light of growing numbers of accusations in the United States and Ireland. But one year later, in June 1993, John Paul II did address clergy sex abuse in a letter to the U.S. bishops. In that letter, which began by drawing attention to the "woes" experienced among the faithful by the scandal of clerical sex abuse, the pope dwelled upon the suffering of the recipients of the letter, the bishops, and in particular their grief and concerns about the crisis, and concluded with a strong criticism of the treatment given to this crisis by the secular media.

Then, in 1994 John Paul II issued *Ordinatio Sacerdotalis*, On Reserving Priestly Ordination to Men Alone, which closed any open discussion in the church, in schools of theology, seminaries, and among bishops in meetings of episcopal conferences and at synods of bishops, about the ordination of women. This document built on the arguments advanced nearly two decades earlier in *Inter Insignores*, a 1976 declaration issued by the Congregation of the Doctrine of the Faith to rebut arguments favoring the ordination of women to priesthood. Soon after *Ordinatio Sacerdotalis* issued in 1994, John Paul II issued in 1995 a *Letter to Women*, which among other things, elaborated a theology of gender complementarity to further validate his defense of a male-only priesthood. This theology developed this pope's 1988 apostolic letter, *Mulieris Dignitatem*, on the Dignity and Vocation of Women, written to coincide with the Fourth World Council on Women sponsored by the United Nations in Beijing that same year.

After John Paul II's death in 2005, his teachings in defense of an all-male priesthood continued to be promoted, unimpeded and unqualified, throughout the papacy of Benedict XVI, until he retired in 2013. Both pontiffs accentuated the sacramental, teaching, and decision-making authority bestowed solely on the parish priest, and also placed restrictions on laypeople in pastoral ministries. In the midst of increasing scrutiny of clergy sexual abuse, as both popes issued public statements on the theology of priesthood and priestly formation, they also issued separate documents defending priestly celibacy and repudiating any consideration of the priestly ordination of women. This cumulative teaching requiring mandatory celibacy and closing further discussion of ordaining women to priestly ordination was further combined with a public doctrine and policy barring the admission of young men with homosexual inclinations to the seminary. This latter policy was linked with the church's lack of openness to discussing homosexuality generally and gay marriage specifically. These recent papal treatments of celibacy, women, gender, and homosexuality—and their interconnections—have, from the beginning, provoked considerable debate and concern among many Catholic theologians, including both critics and staunch defenders of the status quo.[14]

As we have seen, the teachings of John Paul II and Benedict XVI promoted a heroic sacerdotal view of priesthood that strongly implied, if not explicitly assumed, the superiority of male celibate priests to the laity, both male and female. Whether or not it intended to do so, this approach to priesthood undermined the teaching of Vatican II about the equality of all the faithful, the universal call to holiness, and the importance of the faithful's full and active participation in the mission of the church and in lay ministries.[15] And despite Pope Francis's salutary calls for the renewal and reform of priesthood alongside of a dynamic collaboration with the lay faithful, he has not openly expressed any inclination to explore in synodal forums the long-suppressed question of the ordination of women to priesthood. Moreover, without denying his apparently close friendships with individual women over the course of his life, his statements on matters surrounding gender raise questions about how Francis understands gender differences, masculinity and femininity, and the exercise of authority by an all-male clergy and episcopacy not only over laywomen, but over laymen as well.

Nonetheless, in the midst of the crisis brought on by clergy sex abuse and its episcopal cover-up, Francis has received repeated requests to consider ordaining women to priesthood, to the diaconate,[16] and to the episcopacy. He has also received proposals to appoint women (ordained or not) to the cardinalate and to decision-making roles at all levels of the church, from the local parish to the curia. Those advancing these requests may or may not have supported the ordination of women in the past. Many of them argue that priests and bishops, like their male parents, brothers, friends, and coworkers, are inescapably ingrained with patriarchal, and at times hypermasculine, and even misogynist attitudes. These traits are passed on through familial and cultural life, and many argue that they are passed on to an extreme degree in seminary formation and priestly cultures. Analogously, when militaries were exclusively occupied by men, these contexts and cultures created a hothouse for misogynistic attitudes and behaviors; so too in athletics and other associations and professions that have long been dominated by men. The argument goes that including women in seminaries would provide different kinds of voices with different kinds of traits and cultural training.

Arguments from equity have also been voiced. We have limited and fragmentary information on the numbers of females who have been the victims of the clergy sex abuse of minors. A larger question that has not yet been investigated, or at least not been made public, is the number of priests who have formed inappropriate, canonically illicit, or even long-term consensual sexual relationships with women, comparable to intimate sexual relationships with adult men. This information is largely unknown, understudied, and undiscussed. The number of priests and bishops who have had such relationships with adult women (just as with adult men) merits serious consideration when dealing with the larger sets of issues raised by clergy sex abuse.

The sexual exploitation of women religious by priests and bishops also merits greater public attention. Recent investigations have revealed cases where women religious have been treated as subservient slaves who are required to meet the professional, personal, and sexual needs of priests and bishops. If these women religious are not compliant, they suffer the consequences, through various forms of abusive behavior and intimidation. Stories of the oppression of women religious by priests and bishops have been widely reported among members of congregations of women religious, but this information is now receiving greater attention in religious and secular media.[17] The secrecy surrounding the clergy sexual abuse of women religious has been slowly cracked open through victims' testimonies heard and communicated at various levels of the church and publicized through the media in unprecedented ways beginning in 2019. These disclosures have provided further incentives to advocates demanding consideration of the ordination of women to priesthood; but Pope Francis has offered no indication that he is considering taking this major step.

However, in 2016 Pope Francis did establish a study commission to consider the possibility of ordaining women to the diaconate. In a May 2019 report, this group delivered mixed conclusions—not about the historical evidence that women served in diaconal ministries in early Christianity, but about whether these ministries involved sacramental ordination.[18] Whether historical evidence that women deacons were ordained is the only or the best criterion for determining whether this is a viable practice for today has been questioned and debated. A narrow interpretation of past practices need not determine future practices. The argument can be made that introducing this practice is based on a theological argument about the equality, charism, and calling of women as the basis of their being permitted and encouraged to pursue diaconal ministries. The 2019 Amazon Synod urged that women be considered for ordination to the permanent diaconate.[19] But in the end, Pope Francis did not approve the Amazonian bishops' proposals, and offended some by expressing worry in *Querida Amazonia* that ordaining female deacons "would lead us to clericalize women, diminish the great value of what they have already accomplished, and subtly make their indispensable contribution less effective."[20]

With the question of women's ordination to priesthood closed by John Paul II since 1994 and the ordination of women to the diaconate pending further deliberation,[21] it is important to recognize that during this period, some canon lawyers, theologians, and lay pastoral ministers, as well certain bishops and priests throughout the universal church, have continued efforts to make a case for women's ordination, and to promote the placement of nonordained women in leadership and especially in decision-making roles at all levels of the church.

The 1983 Code of Canon Law articulates as a norm the Vatican II teaching that all the baptized faithful, including the clergy, "participate in the threefold ministry of Christ in their own manner and that therefore they are called to exercise the mission which God has entrusted to the Church to fulfil in the world, in accord with the condition proper to each" (CIC §204). Women fully share in this calling. As such they have roles to play in the church's teaching, sanctifying, and governing tasks. Currently, women can be appointed as parish administrators, serve as undersecretary generals of an episcopal conference, as chancellors, notaries, and finance officers of dioceses or religious institutes, as judges in diocesan tribunals or appeal courts, and as officials and senior administrators at the offices of the Roman curia; on February 6, 2021, Pope Francis appointed Sr. Nathalie Becquart undersecretary of the Synod of Bishops. Whether she will vote at the synod has not yet been indicated.[22] Pope Francis has made considerable efforts to place more women in positions of church authority and decision-making: during his papacy a number of women have been appointed undersecretaries in the Vatican curial offices, including the Secretariat of State, Institutes of Consecrated Life and Societies of Apostolic Life, and the Dicastery for Laity, Family and Life, as well as high-ranking positions in other offices.[23] These are significant advances.

Yet even when women have been placed in leadership roles, including in positions where they can exercise decision-making pastoral power, because ordination has remained the prerequisite for full governing power, women are barred from the possibility of exercising binding authority and leadership in relation to priests and bishops. This state of affairs begs the further question: Can one hope for genuine and widespread church reform in these areas when patriarchy and misogyny have been and are still so prevalent among bishops, priests, many men in the church, and in civil society as well? Under these circumstances it is difficult to imagine even incremental progress, much less the dramatic structural changes that many contend are necessary to truly dismantle the conditions and cultures that have contributed to sexual abuse of minors by clergy.

Welcoming Gay Seminarians and Priests?

Homosexuality was one of a variety of issues in sexual ethics that received increased attention during the 1960s as church leaders sought to respond to the so-called sexual revolution taking place in the United States in particular and elsewhere. In 1976 the Vatican's Congregation for the Doctrine of the Faith reiterated the judgment, long held by Catholic moralists, that "homosexual acts are intrinsically disordered."[24] In 1986 Cardinal Joseph Ratzinger (subsequently Pope Benedict XVI), addressed the issue in a pastoral letter, On the Pastoral Care of the Homosexual Person. The letter underscored the respect due to homosexual persons, whose own individual homosexual inclinations Ratzinger wrote, are not in Catholic doctrine held to be sinful as such. Nevertheless, he emphasized that the church must assert that homosexual acts are intrinsically wrong, and the homosexual "inclination itself must be seen as an objective disorder."[25] The 1992 Catechism of the Catholic Church stated that homosexual acts are not only gravely (mortally) sinful, but also intrinsically evil and contrary to natural law.

During the 1960s, as these issues were receiving greater public attention in the United States and Europe, questions about gay seminarians and priests also began to arise. For young Catholic men who were unclear about their sexual orientation or only becoming aware of their attraction to men in a society that was often hostile toward gays, life "in the closet" in seminaries and as ordained priests might have seemed like a reasonable option. But beginning in the late 1980s, the cases of Gilbert Gauthe, John Porter, and John Geoghan raised alarms about clergy abuse of children, and notably boys. And as panic increased surrounding clergy sexual abuse in the Catholic Church in the United States following 2001, many asked whether there was—and despite researchers' findings to the contrary, many assumed—a correlation between homosexual priests and clergy sex abuse of males, especially minors and teenagers.[26]

The 2002 Charter for the Protection of Children called for Apostolic Visitations of U.S. Catholic seminaries by Vatican-appointed bishops and priests (article 17), to evaluate these institutions in terms of how they might be creating the conditions that led to clergy abuse of minors. These visitations took place at seminaries across the United States between September 2005 and July 2006, conducted by bishops, ordained members of religious congregations, and secular clergy. Their aim was to gather data as a basis to address the heightened concerns about clergy abuse of young people following the Boston Globe report in 2002, which it should be recalled pertained to abusive incidents that reached a statistical high point between 1965 and 1985. Among their questions, visiting investigators inquired about the seminarians' sexual ethics courses and whether they were being taught "adequately"—that is, in strict compliance with the *Catechism*, rather than in a way that reflected on the current consensus and debates in the field of theological ethics and among the faithful in parishes and in civil society.

The investigators also sought to gain information about the prevalence of gay seminarians and a so-called gay subculture in seminaries that allegedly promoted homosexuality and homosexual behavior. Not surprisingly, these investigations discovered trends in the seminary population and behavior that reflected the wider culture, but in this case these findings fueled a growing suspicion, and in some cases a moral panic among many that homosexuality was indeed the cause of clergy sex abuse of minors, or at least a crucial contributing factor.

In 2005 the Vatican Congregation for Catholic Education issued an Instruction Concerning the Criteria for the Discernment of Vocations in View of Their Admission to the Seminary and Holy Orders. It reaffirmed the position articulated by Cardinal Ratzinger in his 1986 pastoral letter On the Pastoral Care of the Homosexual Person, that homosexual tendencies are objectively disordered. In light of this and previous church teachings, the 2005 Instruction rendered what seemed to be the logical answer to the question "whether to admit to the seminary and to holy orders candidates who have deep-seated homosexual tendencies"—with a resounding no.

In the ensuing years, this policy has wreaked havoc on the lives of many gay men both currently in and considering applying to the seminary, as well as many gay priests. It is certainly possible to be gay and live a celibate life. Now of course, the "gift" of celibacy may be a spiritual discipline that one must acquire over time, whether in the seminary or after ordination. We have previously remarked on the lack of open discussion and study of sexual relationships between women and ordained priests, whether consenting or not, abusive or not. I noted that as part of discerning the future of mandatory and optional celibacy in the church, we need to acknowledge and examine these relationships much more transparently. A comparable question and a need for transparency pertains to gay men who are in the seminary or ordained. Given the reality that significant numbers of priests and seminarians are not heterosexuals, the current policy, that men with gay sexual orientations should not be in the seminary, creates—or more accurately, perpetuates and further entrenches—a culture of secrecy and lying about these matters. Absent open discussion in seminaries and among gay priests and their bishops, bishops and seminary officials, too, are placed in a very difficult situation.

To be clear: it is not gay priests who are the cause of clergy abuse. Abusive priests who are straight and bisexual have victimized both males and females. The John Jay Report found that a very low percentage of clergy abusers were pedophiles, that is targeting only younger children, male or female. Moreover, the John Jay researchers drawing on extensive literature reviews argued that there is no correlation between gay men, including gay seminarians and priests, and clergy sexual abuse of minors.[27] But current policies in the church have created a culture of secrecy and lying around sexuality that makes it impossible to honestly grapple with the multiple factors that have allowed abuse, and that abets its denial and cover-up.

The Neglected Need: A Realistic Theology of Sexuality and Gender

The crises of clergy sex abuse and episcopal concealment have exposed the reluctance of popes and bishops to openly and honestly address a deeper set of issues pertaining to mandatory celibacy, an all-male clergy, and the reality of same-sex sexual attraction. More than this, these controversies have surfaced a summons to all members of the Catholic Church to face reality, and as a result to fundamentally rethink our understandings and theology of sexuality and gender. Both the opposition to and defense of the current clerical structure raise core issues pertaining to the sexual and bodily character of God's creation of human beings, and the repercussions and refractoriness of these realities as they bear upon human relationships, care and affection, bonds of love, as well as on broader relationships in civil society and religious communities.

The rise of clerical sexual abuse of minors has occurred during a period of intense debate about and dramatic changes in received sexual mores on a variety of fronts, from birth control and cohabitation, to sexual and gender identity, gay and lesbian relationships, partnership and marriage, and a variety of LGBTQ issues. In the face of these changes the hierarchy of the Catholic Church has virtually always staunchly defended traditional positions on sexual ethics, often with a reproachful rhetoric toward those who teach or act otherwise.

What I am calling for here is something more than clearer guidelines against the abuse of minors. We can all agree that abuse is morally repugnant. Beyond this common ground, however, there needs to be a more realistic acknowledgment and more honest conversation among clergy and in seminaries, and among the faith community as a whole, of disputed doctrines in sexual ethics. The same is true about the church's lack of public discussion about women's ordination, its inconsistent hospitality toward LGBTQ people, and the restrictions it places upon their full and active participation as ordained or nonordained ministers in communities of faith. The vast majority of lay theologians are in agreement with the sense of the faithful concerning the need to reconsider and rethink central aspects of the official positions of the church on these issues. Church leaders' lack of openness to honestly discussing and unwillingness to communally discern these matters have significantly contributed to the droves of young people who are currently leaving the church, and to a widely perceived bankruptcy of the church's credibility as a moral teacher.

When seminaries and bishops respond to the abuse crisis by requiring strict compliance on issues of sexual ethics and forbidding open discussion and wider discernment among the faithful, this promotes an authoritarian psychology in seminarians and the newly ordained. It also creates the conditions for an authoritarian ethos in the church that calls into question and threatens priests' capacities to cultivate virtues like humility and compassion, and collaborative skills in listening, collaboration, and community building. More personally, if a seminarian or newly ordained priest does not agree with official Catholic positions on particular issues pertaining to gender, sexuality, and sexual ethics, this context may create a double consciousness: between what I am told I must believe and teach, and what I hold as my own views, questions, evolving positions, which in some cases are contrary to the church's teachings.

Open and honest discussion is needed on these matters at all levels of the church, including in Catholic schools. We need discussion that honors freedom of conscience, and abides by the equality, voice, and authoritative sense of the faithful among all the people of God, with their diversity of receptions and in certain instances dissent from the church's teaching. This is true for all doctrinal areas, but it is especially so in the area of sexuality as it pertains to the church's mission to foster authentic friendship, intimacy, and community building among its members, and for the sake of its own continued vitality.

In short: there must be a profound reappraisal of the official teachings on sexuality in the Catholic Church. Until there is, there will be no real movement forward on the thicket of issues raised by clergy sex abuse of minors, the vulnerable, and of adult women and men. In particular, without dramatic doctrinal developments that advance the full recognition in the church of the equality and authority of all the faithful in relation to the ministerial life of priests, bishops, and in the global hierarchical network of power, we will not attain the radical reform needed to move beyond this crisis. Unless we can advance the leadership of laypeople and especially women in the church, the laments, the grievances, and the unfulfilled aspirations about power and sexuality of the faithful will remain unaddressed, and deep wounds and chronic dysfunctions will remain unhealed. The Catholic Church will remain frozen in time. Only dramatic doctrinal developments and radical reforms can provide the kind transformation necessary to bring about a church with the kind of synodal life and mission dreamed of by Pope Francis.

Conclusion

This chapter has invited the reader to consider what doctrinal, structural, and practical changes are needed in the Catholic Church beyond those already introduced and approved, and how they might address the systemic and cultural factors that have contributed to clergy sex abuse and its episcopal cover-up. Three areas of change have been proposed as catalysts for readers' own further reflection. The first change called for is to remedy the limited and defective realization of the promise of Vatican II to more fully recognize, receive, and implement the equality, voice, and authoritative stance of all the baptized. Consequences of the failure to do this are manifest in the damaged lives of victims, in the malformation and maltreatment of priests, and in the paltry and ineffective engagement of lay leadership with clergy and bishops in collective discernment and decision-making at every level of the church. The second concerns changing the requirements for priestly ordination to include married as well as celibate priests, women as well as men, and acknowledging the callings and gifts of gays and lesbians, whether in sacred unions, or as celibates. The third area, which flows logically from the previous two, concerns the need for a new theology of sexuality and gender in the church.

I ask readers to actively imagine these changes taking place, and to consider what it might mean for the vitality of the church and the promotion of its mission as a living tradition. But we should also consider, what are the realistic prospects of any of these changes actually occurring? And what if none of these changes occur? This leads to the topic of the next and last chapter: In the midst of what will inevitably be ongoing disputes about all these issues, can we find a way together? Is it possible for the church to utilize dialogical procedures, called synods, rooted in the Greek word "a way together," to discern and decide upon a future path that actively incorporates not only the involvement of bishops, but also trained theologians, clergy and lay, and beyond that, representatives of the sense of all the faithful? Can we find a way together? If this proves impossible, what will this mean for the future of the church?

Chapter 6

Can We Find a Way Together?

This question calls to mind Pope Francis's use of the term *synodality*, which is central to his vision for the church and its future. This term captures the heart of the message of Vatican II in which all the people of God, laypeople, bishops, and theologians, listen to and learn from each other as they make their ways together in their pilgrimage of faith.[1] This chapter addresses the challenge of advancing synodality in a wounded and wounding church.

The particular question I am posing here, and that many other Catholics are asking now, is *"Can we find a way together?"* Is it even possible? As we have seen, many Catholics, especially today in light of the clergy sex abuse scandal, have been so deeply wounded by the church's many forms of dysfunction that they seriously doubt it. As we've also discussed, these doubts spring not only from the sex abuse scandal but also from problems with a much longer history in the Catholic Church. The cumulative effect has been dramatic: increasing numbers of people leaving the church, abandoning long-habituated practices of the faith, and losing the deep moorings once provided by a shared Catholic imagination saturated by the symbols and narratives of the liturgy, Scriptures, creed, and spiritual practices and commitments to works of mercy and work for justice.

With this question as my framework, and against the backdrop of all we have considered up to this point, I will, in this final chapter, defend the following thesis: If we want to find a way together, as Pope Francis has advocated and as I do, it is imperative that we promote dialogue in the church through participatory structures such as councils, synods, and other assemblies that foster free speech and courageous honesty, thereby empowering the faithful at all levels to speak together about the pressing challenges, controversies, and conflicts confronting the church today.

To bring to life this vibrant dialogical vision, one of the most pressing and demanding tasks will be to establish new ways for the lay faithful to join with theologians in collaboration with bishops to exercise their collective baptismal rights and duties, their Spirit-given charisms, and their well-developed talents in actively contributing to discernment and decision-making processes in the church. By so doing, the people of God in the synodal church can engage their creative imaginations with their critical reason to address prophetically the church's problems and dysfunctions and to envision, together, a way forward. Bishops, long the sole executive authorities in the church, are unaccustomed to working collaboratively with laypeople and theologians; for laypeople and theologians, genuine collaboration with bishops is also unfamiliar territory. Given this, there will be a need for considerable experimentation, not to mention patience, on the way to forging a genuinely synodal church.

If we are to move meaningfully toward this synodal, dialogical way of being church, what might be the most promising directions to take? To consider our options, I will introduce three different pathways.

The first is *the synodal way* promoted explicitly by Pope Francis. Three recent examples will help illustrate this synodal way in action: a diocesan synod conducted in Limerick, Ireland, a plenary council currently underway in Australia, and a provocative approach being developed in Germany called the synodal way. Each provides opportunities for laypeople, theologians, and bishops to listen to one another and, together, to consider the pressing issues and opportunities facing the church in the current time and to begin to imagine how these issues might be addressed.

Second, we will briefly explore *the way of restorative justice*, which provides a process for victim-survivors to address unresolved issues associated with the moral injuries they have suffered, often by meeting their assailants in an attempt to find some measure of resolution that the legal justice system cannot provide.

Our third example, which will also conclude this book, is *the way of seekers at the margins*. This is a path being pursued by some who remain at the margins within the church and some who are at the margins outside the church. Many of these people have been hurt, angered, and frustrated by the actions of clergy and bishops; some have become disaffiliated from the church in their hearts, and others in practice. But rather than sitting back or completely walking away, these disaffected Catholics, many of them younger, are seeking and finding different, sometimes more radical contexts for exploring and expressing their Christian faith and action. For some this may mean the *way of* particular ecclesial communities or *movements* such as base Christian communities, which are widespread in Latin America and Africa; Jesuit-affiliated Christian Life Community, which has a wide membership around the world; or the international Focolare movement. These people may remain affiliated with the institutional church (and in spirit if not always in practice with their parish, diocese, and bishop), even as they engage in lay-led groups or movements whose more intentional forms of spiritual practices, works of mercy, and work for justice are a plea for more radical reforms in the church at large.

Other seekers on the margins pursue more radical ways of reform of life and action outside of any organized church movement or organization. For these people, institutional disaffiliation is a necessary part of their struggle against a church dominated by an all-male hierarchical governance that cannot make room for more open discussion and debate about pressing issues raised by clergy sex abuse. In varying ways, these seekers at the margins pursue a viable Catholic form of spirituality—Catholic in spirit if not always in letter—that is frequently marked by active engagement with works of mercy and work for justice.

The Synodal Way

Synodal processes undertaken within the contemporary Catholic Church have been devoted to a variety of pressing issues, such as on ecology and environmental issues, marriage and family, and young people. Each of the synodal examples that we will consider were convened in locations—Ireland, Australia, and Germany—that struggled with issues raised by clergy sex abuse and episcopal cover-ups and intentionally sought to address those issues.

As we consider these three, I am particularly interested in the question of whether there is room for acknowledging conflict and fostering candid honesty in these kinds of synodal forums. Do these synodal procedures create a space for open discussion about contested issues? Do they encourage or stifle people who seek to speak out on sensitive or controversial matters? Are participants allowed to propose, deliberate, and vote on positions that are contrary to the official teachings and policies of the church? And to what extent does all of this get reflected in public tallies conveying the results of synodal deliberations?

Limerick Diocesan Synod

Let us begin with the 2014–16 Limerick Diocesan Synod. Limerick, the third largest diocese in Ireland after Dublin and Cork, comprises 60 parishes, roughly 170,000 Catholics, and 105 priests. Ten priests have allegedly been involved in the sexual abuse of minors since 1960, but none of these men has been criminally convicted, and some have since died. Bishop Donal Murray, installed in 1996, was accused of not adequately handling an accusation against a priest during his time in Dublin. Murray denied the charges of cover-up but ultimately resigned in 2009. All of this seriously undermined the trust of the members in the bishop of the diocese.

One month after Pope Francis's inauguration, a new bishop, Brendan Leahy, was installed in Limerick on April 14, 2013. One of Bishop Leahy's first acts was to call a Limerick Diocesan Synod, in the document "Together in Mission, A Time to Begin Again," on

September 28, 2014. When he announced that this synod was to take place, clergy sex abuse of children loomed large in the bishop's review of the issues that had influenced the recent period in the diocese's history.

> Above all, members of the Church have experienced bewilderment because of revelations of the horrible deeds done to children in our midst. I don't think it's too strong to say there has been an ecclesial trauma and that it has shaken all of us. It has made us ask: What was going on? How did things go so wrong? Can it be that we drifted so far from the Gospel? Healing and renewal are never automatic. They take time and we need to give each other room for that process to begin. A Synod will be a place for naming the wounds that have traumatized children and their families and the entire Church-body. It will also be a place for us to understand the further healing we have to give and what we need to do so we can all embark on a new journey together in trust and faith.[2]

Along with the specific issues that a synod would enable the faithful of Limerick to address, especially clergy abuse of minors and the controversy surrounding the previous bishop, the synod was designed to begin a new chapter in the diocese. The abundance of information generated during the synod on the diocesan website suggests that this synod was well designed, well executed, and productive, and there is a strong indication that challenging issues were raised and aired.[3] In launching the synod, Bishop Brendan Leahy actively invited such openness:

> The Synod will need to provide forums where people can discuss the dark issues and the practical problems, their disappointments and their inner search....But it is not enough to name problems. We will need to discern together what is the Holy Spirit suggesting to us today. And we need to have confidence that the Spirit is with us! Difficulties are never the last word in the Christian vocabulary.[4]

The synod process engaged over five thousand people in a listening process that included children and the elderly. There were four thousand people who responded to a questionnaire distributed in April 2015 with the purpose of identifying issues that merited attention at the synod; there were also involved 1,500 individuals from all sixty parishes in the diocese and members of twenty-five other groups, including educators at all levels: primary, secondary, and tertiary, health-care workers, migrants, and the disabled. On Delegate Day in the first week of October 2015, the four hundred delegates, 70 percent of whom were laypeople, gathered in forums to discuss and discern the twelve top issues and to select the top six themes for the Synod: (1) Community and Sense of Belonging; (2) Faith Formation; (3) Pastoral Care of the Family; (4) New Models of Leadership; (5) Liturgy and Life; and (6) Young People. The final synod assembly gathered for three days in April 2016 to establish a course of action.

The data from the April 2016 synod assembly was assessed by Bishop Leahy assisted by a working group composed of Father Eamonn Fitzgibbon, the synod director, and experts in social research, research methodology, and pastoral planning, all trained to interpret the synod data. Bishop Leahy issued his final synod report, "Moving Forward Together in Hope," on December 8, 2016. This upbeat, forward-looking statement is accompanied by a well-designed plan based on the discussions over the years of the synodal process and the votes of the four hundred in attendance at the final synod assembly. Bishop Leahy's introduction states positively the aspirations of synodality: "Throughout our preparation for the Synod, the whole Diocese has been learning together to be 'synodal,' that is, walking together, journeying together, with Jesus among us, as we move forward in hope." In the closing pages of his inspirational statement, Bishop Leahy writes that "it is one of the great tricks of the Devil to make us confuse a false humility with what in reality is a temptation against hope. A false humility makes us see only our imperfections and sins, challenges and difficulties and stop there.... This false humility is, in reality, a temptation against hope."[5]

The diocesan website reports that in group discussions, synod participants expressed concerns about reaching out to those hurt by the church, with some mention of those struggling with the aftermath of clergy sex abuse. However, there is no evidence that these discussions addressed causes of clergy sexual abuse and other problems in the church; in particular, there is no evidence that clericalism or the challenges posed by how episcopal authority have been discussed during the synod. Considerable concerns were expressed about the need for greater participation of women and all of the laity in the church, in liturgy, and in church governance, and these were reflected in both the voting that took place and in the strategic plan that was issued. And judging by the final documents in 2016 and the progress report posted in 2017 on the diocesan website, many reasonable expressions of these positive avenues promoting a lay-led church are being explored and developed in the Limerick Diocese.

However, one might also get the impression that there was an attempt to move beyond, without genuinely addressing, lingering concerns associated with clergy abuse and the challenging issues pertaining to the misuse of power. The question can be asked: Despite some good outcomes, have deeper and still-unresolved problems and conflicts facing the Limerick Diocese been marginalized and avoided in this synodal process? One could wonder if, at times, efforts to raise these deeper, more structural problems may have been dismissed or mistakenly interpreted as instances of the "false humility" that subverts hope. Without denying the considerable assets of the Limerick Synod, it remains to be seen whether a forward-looking synodal vision can be combined with a realistic assessment of structural difficulties facing the church and an honest exploration of possible ways of addressing them.

Australian Plenary Council

A second illustration of the synodal way is provided by the Australian Plenary Council, which was launched in 2018, the year after the Australian Royal Commission published its final report on a 2015–17 investigation into "Institutional Responses to Child Sexual Abuse." This report determined that between 1980 and 2015, about 4,500 claims of child sexual abuse took place and allegations were made against 1,880 Catholic clergy. Convened in 2018—in part in response to the crisis of trust these revelations provoked—the Australian plenary council is scheduled to complete its work in 2022. As a formal plenary council, this event is identified in canon law as a synodal procedure.

The council's first phase was an immense, nationwide undertaking, much larger than any diocesan synod, which has actively included participants who are marginalized or disaffiliated members of the Australian Catholic Church. During the initial, "listening phase," over 222,000 participants made their views known by answering questionnaires or participating in group dialogues. The findings from this data were provided on a website report on phase one, *Listen to What the Spirit is Saying*, a three hundred–plus-page document that describes every one of the issues that received attention at this stage of the Plenary Council, features individual statements by people, and provides personal anecdotal narratives illustrating each main topic.[6]

An entire section of the report was devoted to clergy sexual abuse of children and the 2017 Royal Commission's report on this topic, with council participants issuing a major call for an implementation of the Royal Commission's recommendations with greater concern for victim-survivors. Among the many voices recorded, one hears calls for healing and moving beyond the scandal, but also repeated mentions of the role played by clericalism and devoted some attention to the cover-up of abuse by bishops.

The first-phase document further reports that many participants favor ending mandatory celibacy, ordaining women priests and married men (and, in principle, married women too), and, above all, encouraging greater involvement of the laity, especially women, in church ministries and administration, and much more open discussion of sexual morality and LGBTQ issues. The second phase of the plenary council, during 2019–20, is devoted to listening and discernment on national themes culled from the first phase. Phase Two will pave the way for the Assembly of the Plenary Council that will be held in two parts, at this writing currently scheduled to take place October 3–10, 2021, and the second July 4–9, 2022.[7]

At the end of Phase One an orienting question and six themes were selected to be treated next in dialogue and discernment groups and formulated in statements during Phase Two: "How is God calling us to be a Christ-centered Church that is: [1] missionary and evangelizing; [2] inclusive, participatory, and synodal; [3] prayerful and eucharistic; [4] humble, healing, and merciful; [5] a joyful, hope-filled, and servant community; and [6] open to conversion, renewal, and reform?"

One major challenge facing the plenary council concerns the range of issues that participants have raised that press against the church's business-as-usual: about the ordination of married and women priests; about how clericalism can be overcome; about how to meaningfully address complicity by bishops with allegedly abusive behavior by priests; and about how the laity and especially women can exercise their baptismal authority in liturgy and decision-making in the church.

If the plenary council concludes with proposals for renewal that leave the status quo in these areas unchanged, this large-scale synodal process could yield new waves of disappointment and increasing disaffection with the church.[8] This process has started so well; will it end poorly? And what would be required for the plenary assembly to end well? Will those who raised hard questions influence the synod's outcomes in unpredictable ways, or will their questions and proposals for change be rejected? And if the latter, will these people still feel like important participants who have left their mark on the council's outcome? Might they nonetheless contribute to a new groundswell of reform and renewal in the Australian Catholic Church, even if it is not as they imagined?

German Synodal Way

Our third example is the German Synodal Way. This project is a joint undertaking of the German Bishops' Conference and an organization of laypeople called the Central Committee of German Catholics, a lay Catholic association that arose during the mid-nineteenth century to regularly discuss and address important church and civic issues.[9]

Originally inspired and launched by the Würzburg Synod that took place between 1971 and 1975, for over four decades the "joint conference" of the German Episcopal Conference and the Central Committee has met twice a year to discuss important issues at gatherings comprised of ten representatives from the Bishops' Conference and ten laypeople from the Central Committee. The Synodal Way, a project of the joint conference, emerged as a response to a major scientific report commissioned by the German Bishops' Conference to analyze instances of clergy sexual abuse that took place in the twenty-seven dioceses of Germany between 1946 and 2014. The report, released in 2018, cited more than 38,000 cases of abuse in Germany, committed by about 1,700 Catholic clerics during the seven decades studied. Catholics in Germany were horrified by these revelations.

In 2019 the German Bishops' Conference confirmed that during the previous year, 272,771 Catholics had left the church. In the face of the scandal and Catholics' response to it, the German bishops decided that a nationwide deliberative process among Catholics, to discuss the pertinent issues and search for solutions, was urgently needed. Organizing a national synod for this purpose, they judged, would take too long. An unconventional model was thus devised in which German bishops would collaborate with members of the Central Committee to identify and address issues raised by the report. This endeavor began on the first day of Advent, December 1, 2019, and was scheduled to last for two years.

This joint conference of German bishops and the Central Committee devised a structure to ensure that bishops, laypeople, and theologians engaged in collaborative decision-making to address the challenges facing the church in Germany. The developed structure culminates with a Synodal Assembly composed of a total number of 227 members with voting rights with 69 German bishops and 69 laypeople from the Central Committee with decision-making authority. Four synodal forums, composed of bishops and laypeople, were chosen to prepare documents on key issues. These documents are scheduled to be discussed, revised, and finally voted upon by the forums, the synodal assembly, and synodal leadership administrators. All of these members have voting rights. Those appointed to serve on the Synodal Assembly included 105 clerics (69 bishops, 32 priests, and 4 deacons) and 122 laypeople, including 70 women.[10]

The four forum groups, which include theologians, were composed of no more than ten bishops appointed by the German Bishops' Conference and ten lay members chosen by the Central Committee. The forum membership, varying in size from eleven to twenty, was approved by the Synodal Assembly. Each forum group was charged with separately preparing a position paper on one of these topics: (1) Power and the Separation of Powers in the Church—Shared Participation and Involvement in Mission, (2) Living in Successful Relationships—Living Love in Sexuality and Partnership, (3) Priestly Existence Today, and (4) Women in Ministries and Offices in the Church.

The Bishops' Conference and the Central Committee explicitly envisioned and described this endeavor as a "binding synodal process" that would entail mutual listening and collective discernment and decision-making among participating bishops and laypeople, including theologians. In other words, this Synodal Way was to be not simply the bishops' consultative process with theologians and laypeople, but an exercise in collaborative ecclesial decision-making.

In the Vatican, the formula "binding synodal process" raised concerns among the cardinal prefects of three important Curial Congregations: Marc Ouellet, the Congregation for the Bishops; Louis Ladaria, the Congregation of the Doctrine of the Faith; and Beniamino Stella, the Congregation for the Clergy, along with Cardinal Pietro Parolin, the Vatican Secretary of State. They called into question both the German bishops' decision and their authority to seek a binding agreement with representatives of the lay Central Committee. The Vatican officials expressed their concerns to Pope Francis, who in response decided to write a letter to the people of God in Germany about the proposed German synodal procedure.

In his letter, released on June 29, 2019, Pope Francis expressed his care for the German people of God and their future and his desire that God give them the help they needed to move forward. He accentuated the need for spiritual conversion, emphasizing that structural reform offers no solution if it is not guided by the Spirit and grace. His remarks certainly distinguished, and could be interpreted as dichotomizing, the influence of the Spirit and structural reform. Francis further wrote, "What [the Synodal Way] means concretely and how it develops will certainly have to be considered even more deeply."

While sounding notes of caution, the pope's letter did not foreclose the possibility of the German bishops conducting a synodal process in collaboration with the Central Committee of German Catholics. Strictly speaking, their proposed endeavor corresponds with what Francis calls in his letter a form of "synodality from the bottom up." Still, the pope insists that "synodality... [which] comes from above downward...is the only way to make mature decisions in matters essential to the faith and life of the Church."[11] And he repeats what he said to the German bishops in their *ad limina* meeting in 2015 "that one of the first and greatest temptations in the church sphere is to believe that the solutions to current and future problems can be accomplished solely by way of the reform of structures, organizations, and administration, but that in the end in no way touch the vital points that actually need attention."[12] To do so requires a spiritual mode of discernment and the gift of the Holy Spirit.

Two months after Francis wrote his letter, on September 4, Cardinal Ouellet wrote to Cardinal Reinhard Marx to express concerns that the proposed Synodal Way was not in compliance with the requirements of a synod as stipulated in canon law. In response, the German bishops clarified further details about this Synodal Way at their September 23–26, 2019, Episcopal Conference. This Synodal Way, the bishops explained, is neither an official diocesan synod nor a national synod in the canonical sense that allows for consulting but no final voting by lay participants. Nor is it a plenary or provincial council that engages all the faithful with the bishops and includes a consultative vote from all participants. It is, the bishops asserted, sui generis.[13] In addition, the bishops introduced language into the statutes about passing the final decisions of the synodal assembly. "The resolutions require a two-thirds majority of the members present, which includes a two-thirds majority of the members present of the German Bishops' Conference."[14]

On November 22, 2019, the statutes were approved by the Central Committee, after considerable debate among the members, by a vote of seventeen with five abstentions. It had been made clear that the Synodal Way's resolutions will have no binding power in the universal church, nor by application to the bishops' conference; nor will these resolutions apply to decisions of local bishops pertaining to the local church. In the words of the Statutes of the Synodal Way, "Resolutions of the Synodical Assembly have no legal effect of their own accord. The authority of the Bishops' Conference and of the individual diocesan bishops to issue legal norms and exercise their teaching authority (magisterium) within the respective spheres of responsibilities remains unaffected by the resolutions."[15]

This revised statute could be judged as jettisoning the promise of reaching binding synodal resolutions, yet some have suggested that there still can be movement beyond the common impasse over the discernment of the laity, theologians, and the bishops in these synodal procedures. Karin Kortmann, the vice president of the Central Committee, "expressly rejected criticism of the alleged non-binding nature of the decision-making possibilities of the Synodal Way. It is not the statutes that fall short here, they merely depict what church law stipulates. She promised, 'We will do everything we can to reach binding resolutions and votes in the Synodal Assembly.'"[16]

Each of the four documents developed by the forums of bishops, theologians, and lay members addresses difficult contested issues and responds to challenging questions and criticisms about official doctrines and policies; each has the opportunity to offer alternative approaches. It remains to be seen how these four documents and the final votes they receive will contribute to any binding authority they might have on ecclesial practice in local German churches going forward. And, as Karin Kortmann noted, countering certain interpretations of Pope Francis's letter to the German people: "Let us not persuade ourselves of a supposedly incompatible antagonism of structural reforms and spiritual deepening."[17]

In closing this section, I simply observe that in the United States nothing comparable to these synods has taken place between 1985 and 2020; no diocesan or national forum has been devoted to providing an opportunity for all the faithful, explicitly including theologians, to gather in synod assemblies with bishops to address the topic of the clergy sexual abuse of minors and episcopal concealment, and to deliberate together over how to address its causes and consequences.

The Way of Restorative Justice

Restorative justice has emerged over the last fifty years as a way to address the harm inflicted on individuals and communities as a result of behavior that is abusive, aggressive, and at times legally criminal, from bullying in schools to violence in war, and also including unwanted sexual behavior and sexual abuse. In cases of criminal behavior, restorative justice offers an alternative way, for some as a complement and for others a substitute, to standard approaches to conflict negotiation and civil and criminal justice, providing a way to grapple with such questions as, "What harm has been done? What needs have arisen and whose obligation is it to meet those needs?" And more poignantly, from victims to perpetrators, "Why did you do this to me? How could you do this to me?"[18]

In the 1990s this approach began to be adapted for and adopted in cases of sexual violence, including the sexual abuse of children by Catholic clergy. This process of communication, conducted with the offender at the initiative of the victim, is mediated by professionals, in certain cases accompanied by family members and representatives of communities of care of both the victim and the offender.

Restorative justice methods aim to help victim-survivors understand the offender's motivation, to make clear to the offender the kinds of harm the offender has inflicted, and to enable the victim-survivor to witness the offender's acknowledgment that this abusive behavior did in fact take place. The perpetrator's public acknowledgment of the abuse helps confirm that the victim is genuinely a survivor and not just a victim of the abuser's actions. The process can involve the survivor's expression of forgiveness of the abuser, but this is neither required nor presumed. The victim-survivor may also seek agreements with the offender concerning accountability and reparation.

The way of restorative justice provides resources that victim-survivors can use to offset many obstacles and limitations that the legal justice system entails. For example, in Ireland, the United States, and Australia, the common-law tradition features an adversarial approach to accuser and defendant, and one in which the prosecuting attorney in criminal lawsuits has to prove beyond a reasonable doubt that the alleged crime occurred, and yet a verdict against an alleged assailant can in certain lawsuits be dismissed by the judge on a technicality. Trials can be punishing for victim-accusers, and they are regularly inconclusive and profoundly disappointing for the victim making the legal allegation.

Restorative justice provides a moral framework that is deeply rooted in Indigenous American traditions, the Christian tradition, and other religious traditions. It is philosophically coherent and therapeutically informed, and it upholds two sets of contrasting and contested claims: On one hand, restorative justice defends and recognizes a morally appropriate, righteous, justifiable form of anger as virtuous for individuals and communities.[19] This can be clearly distinguished from anger that seeks retribution and revenge, such anger that can justify inflicting and escalating harm. On the other hand and simultaneously, restorative justice offers a victim-survivor a way to begin the process of forgiving the abuser and perhaps even a path toward reconciliation. It acknowledges, however, that forgiveness and reconciliation may be understandably difficult if not impossible for the victim-survivor to desire or achieve. Forgiveness and reconciliation are not simple decisions but, in some sense, gifts from God; restorative justice procedures may provide conducive circumstances for these to take place, but they are neither the primary nor the necessary outcomes. And the victim-survivor is under no such obligation and should not be pressured to forgive the assailant. Instead, restorative justice provides a possible avenue for addressing the harm done, and can contribute to a restorative, healing process. Still, depending on the kinds and levels of damage inflicted by the abusive behavior, even these outcomes may not be attained.

A victim-survivor often suffers from various psychic difficulties: depression, anger, anxiety, self-hatred, self-abusive behavior, substance abuse, suicidal ideation, and dissociation.[20] These are manifestations of the moral injury done to the individual. These criminal acts may also harm the person's relationships with others—parents, siblings, teachers, friends, and more, and may also damage communities and institutions. Most profoundly for some, it regularly happens that the victim's relationship with God is profoundly impaired if not irreparably destroyed.

Restorative justice concentrates on the personal character of abusive behavior and on the individual victim-survivor in relation to the accused. The offender, in Catholic contexts, is usually an individual priest in a parish or in a school. Bishops and provincials are not often intended interlocutors, but a significant number of them have learned the importance of meeting with victim-survivors, hearing their stories, and discovering the many ways in which people in positions of hierarchical authority have contributed to victims' brokenness and bear some responsibility.

Yet the way of restorative justice for addressing clergy sexual abuse also raises further, more systemic questions. Can a comprehensive healing process take place for the victim, or possibly even the offender, without other factors that have influenced priestly formation and the practices whereby credibly accused abusive priests were reassigned to different churches, schools, or other institutions? Can real healing take place without bringing into the process bishops and provincials who supervised individual clergy abusers, acknowledging these authority figures' relation to the national and global networks of power exercised by bishops and religious superiors, and posing to these men some of the agonized questions voiced by victims, such as, "Why did you make it possible for me to be abused?" "What can you and your fellow bishops or provincials in your religious order do to address the suffering I have endured and the wounds that I have been subjected to, often repeatedly, because of what you have done or not done?"

Such questions are awkward and painful, but they also are legitimate and even necessary. Answering them would require bishops and provincials to examine their own complicity in creating and sustaining an organizational culture in the church that has maintained a code of silence and concealment that enabled abuse to go unchecked and unpunished.

As valuable as the way of restorative justice is for some individuals, and acknowledging the ripple effects of healing it can have for the web of relationships in which abused people participate, is there not something in addition to restorative justice that is needed, something beyond civil or criminal or canonical legal procedures? In an effort to promote the development of new cultures and practices of accountability and responsibility, the February 2019 Vatican meeting of episcopal leaders of bishops' conferences from around the world represented a step in the right direction. But what more local roles can diocesan, provincial, and plenary synods and councils play in this movement toward a culture of mutual accountability and responsibility, so necessary for the healing of Catholic communities?

To my knowledge, victim-survivors of clergy sex abuse and their families and friends currently have no process for pursuing a way of restorative justice with bishops and superiors of religious orders whose acts of complicity and concealment have perpetuated—and allowed abusers to evade responsibility or penalties for inflicting—such destructive forms of behavior on individuals, their loved ones, and their wider communities.

To remedy this lack will require expanding practices of restorative justice to include meetings between victim-survivors and bishops, religious superiors, and perhaps in some instances even the pope. But on their own, even these meetings cannot suffice. They must be complemented by synodal ways that allow for the practice of free and honest speech and that enable members of the church together to discern not just the personal factors that have contributed to abuse, but also the cultural and systemic dynamics that must be identified and addressed.

The Way of Seekers at the Margins

In the midst of the constellation of church controversies and conflicts that marks this age, many people, frequently young people, find themselves at the margins of the Catholic Church. Some hover at the margins within the church, conflicted, dissatisfied, yet still participating to some degree in the sacraments and possibly in church activities. Others linger at the margins on the outside of the church, disaffiliated and disengaged from its life and mission. The increasing numbers of these marginalized Catholics can't be attributed to modern forms of secularism and individualism entirely, even though no one can escape their influences. This phenomenon is at least as much, and likely to a larger degree, the result of difficulties taking place in the church.

Many people who self-identify as disaffiliated still admit a belief in God, an inchoate desire for God, and in some cases an active relationship with God. Some concede they are seekers who have a hunger for spirituality and a community in which they can share with others their wonder, awe, and gratitude in their life, and some as well speak about occasions of deep sadness, melancholy, remorse, and anguish that convey a deep hunger for more, for connection with others and perhaps with a God who is transcendent and immanent in our relationships with others, nature, and the cosmos. Those seekers who have lost patience with the church sometimes combine their deeper spiritual desires with a passion for active engagement with those in need, the poor, the sick, and the hungry associated with works of mercy, as well as those who are engaged in work for justice who advance cultural and systemic change in the interests of promoting racial, gender, economic, and environmental justice.

On this third path one also encounters people who long for doctrinal changes and ecclesial reforms that people do not discuss at church. This motivates some seekers, whether they remain active within the church or not, to piece together discerning, individual forms of life that remain profoundly Catholic in principle but often not in institutional identification. Taking this path enables many seekers at the margins to discover or rediscover and exhibit a Catholic imagination and an embodied sense of piety that the church's leaders have damaged and betrayed.

How can people live with this sense of being wounded and disoriented at this moment in the church? Surveys indicate that many living on the margins of the church continue to profess core beliefs of the faith, but a significant percentage have been infuriated by the failures of bishops and priests in addressing clergy abuse, clericalism, and hierarchicalism, and reject the church's restrictions on who can be ordained, the role of the laity in church ministry and leadership, as well as various teachings in sexual ethics that also seem related to the underlying causes of the problems that the sexual abuse crisis has exposed.[21]

In fact, the church's theological tradition provides resources for addressing many contemporary Catholics' ambivalence toward and even rejection of certain teachings. In this regard, three basic types or levels of doctrine in the church are identified in theology.[22] Certain beliefs are central core convictions of faith, known as official dogmas of the Catholic faith, and these are identified as the highest level of doctrine, associated above all with creedal convictions. A second level of church teaching is identified as definitive doctrine, which includes teachings held as necessary to support other dogmatic teachings, such as the officially designated books included in the canon of the Sacred Scripture, which was explicitly taught at the Council of Trent.

A third level of teaching is identified as authoritative doctrine and includes moral teachings that are customarily associated with modern Catholic social teachings officially taught through papal encyclical letters and by bishops; these doctrines are based on teachings of Scripture, doctrinal and theological tradition, including the esteemed contributions of theologians, especially Thomas Aquinas and his heirs. These doctrines are acknowledged as authoritative, or respected, but have at times been wrongly identified as infallible or irreformable, but in fact it is widely and correctly acknowledged among bishops, priests, theologians, and educated Catholics that these teachings are potentially fallible and therefore susceptible to development.

For most believers, even those with serious reservations concerning specific moral teachings or church practices, the center—the core beliefs—holds, even with disputes about interpretations and qualifications, and despite more basic questions and doubts about doctrines held as authoritative but not infallible and irreformable. Vatican II introduced the formula "hierarchy of truths" to express this traditional affirmation of shared core beliefs in relation to disputed interpretations of core beliefs and disputed beliefs between Catholic, Orthodox, and Protestant churches. After the council, this category was used to address the faith experience among believers in the Catholic Church and in other churches as well.[23]

Eminent twentieth-century theologian Karl Rahner, SJ, who played an important role as advisor to the bishops at Vatican II, commended the importance of the council's teaching about the hierarchy of truth. Rahner also argued that without denying the core creedal faith of Catholics, individuals inevitably formulate in their imaginations their own concrete catechism, which reflects what could be called their own personal hierarchy of truths, shaped by their own form of spirituality and popular piety that informs how these doctrines are understood and applied to everyday life.[24] Believers embrace creedal foundations of faith but inevitably interpret them, their significance, practical implications, and applications in different ways.

A second kind of theological resource for Catholics dealing with conflicts and controversies in the church comes from the ecumenical movement. In the decades that followed Vatican II, informed by countless dialogues among Catholics, Orthodox, and Protestants, Catholic ecumenists Margaret O'Gara and Paul Murray championed a theological orientation that has become known as "receptive ecumenism." This approach affirms that there can be "a mutual exchange of gifts" between different communities of faith as they share their distinctive receptions and interpretations of core beliefs, and that such reciprocity between church communions can provide ways for each faith community to address certain limitations and even expressions of woundedness and dysfunctions within their own churches. To this end, in 1999, Lutherans and Catholics officially agreed that there can be a "differentiated consensus" among Christian communities based on past affirmations about core beliefs, such as how we understand basic beliefs about Christian faith, justification, and sanctification. Respected Lutheran theologian Theodor Dieter has argued not only that we can recognize a differentiated consensus among us about core beliefs, but that there can also be a differentiating consensus as we continue to strive for and grow into a deeper understanding and application of these beliefs.[25]

These kinds, types, or levels of teachings and these theological formulas—hierarchy of truths and differentiated consensus—provide different ways for individuals and groups to think about their own questions, doubts, and disagreements about these teachings. These various recognized approaches to Catholic teachings and policies indicate that there are different avenues by which seekers at the margins can embrace their convictions about the importance of freely exercising their informed consciences as they discern and make decisions about matters of faith in action in everyday life. Both the teaching on the hierarchy of truths and the advancement of receptive ecumenism make room for disagreement about certain kinds of teaching and how they might be interpreted and applied differently, and how one can reasonably expect dissent in matters of faith and morals.

How might these approaches to different levels of church teaching and between people with different points of view help those struggling with their involvement or lack of involvement in the Catholic Church today? Often, people who are on the margins find themselves justifiably apprehensive about participating in certain church communities because of how certain teachings and their authoritative weight are interpreted and accentuated. On issues of gender orientation and same-sex unions, for instance, priests and bishops can have a style of teaching and leadership that can alienate Catholics and especially young people, especially if they themselves are gay or they have loved ones who are. When one holds the core beliefs of the church and believes that there is a legitimate plurality and diversity in matters of faith, seekers can find warrants for searching out faith communities that affirm core beliefs of the creedal faith, but that also provide space and time for members to discern and discover diverse ways of interpreting and applying these convictions and negotiating disputed issues in the church.

Drawing on these theological resources, and honestly admitting faith struggles and the aspirations for a genuine faith-in-action among seekers, is it possible to imagine that seekers at the margins might be encouraged to participate in a synodal way that might let them speak their mind and express their protests, which could also influence wider circles of people in the church?

What would entice seekers to become involved in synodal ways and what might be gained? All Catholics, whether active, alienated, or disaffiliated, would need to be offered the space and training in basic practices for discerning the sense of faith in one's personal life, but also the invitation to think about the sense of the faith of the community. This would mean finding ways to explicitly honor the efforts of seekers at the margins who are also striving to discern the sense of the faith in their own personal lives, and to honor the collective discernment of the sense of the faithful taking place in diverse communities of faith, even in the face of discord and conflict.

In pursuing this path, all the faithful must grow into a realization that Pope John XXIII expressed days after he convoked the Second Vatican Council in January 1959 when he cited a quotation of long-disputed origin: "In essentials unity, in doubtful things liberty, in all things charity."[26] But the question has sometimes been raised, what is essential and what is doubtful? And the customary response is to say that dogmatic teachings are essential, but on issues of morals and practical matters of application there may be doubts and even disagreements about what is binding. Yet in matters of receiving, interpreting, and applying church teachings and policies there may be questions and doubts and disagreements about all manner of teachings and policies.

Drawing on the spiritual wisdom and idioms of Pope Francis and his contemporaries, perhaps there is a need for a new aphorism: in matters of conflict, practice honesty; when confronting oppositions, pursue convergences; and where hostilities persist, identify legitimate dissent while embracing differentiated consensus and encouraging differentiating consensus. Along the way we must admit that not all seekers will find a community of faith in their pursuit of a spiritual purpose in freedom that enables works of mercy and work for justice, at least not always a Catholic community. But we can hope that they will find companions and communities to support them as they continue their seeking.

Conclusion

We might wish we had the definitive answer to the question: Can we find a way together in the midst of this era of clergy sex abuse? There are no simplistic answers, but these three pathways are providing, for many, a measure of healing and hope, and ways forward. As Catholics continue to grapple with the controversies and conflicts we have considered here, the most promising option will be to find ways for these three pathways to intersect and converge.

The clerical and episcopal matrix of power in the global church has been instrumental in creating the conditions for this wounded and wounding church. Pope Francis has sought to purge, purify, and reform the church by advancing synodality and a sound decentralization in the church, while also advancing a polycentric approach to the church. His convictions and program are rooted in a belief and confidence in God's desire to work through bishops (and no doubt also provincials of religious orders), individually and collectively in episcopal conferences and various forms of synods, attentively listening to and learning from the sense of the faithful people of God as they exercise their episcopal and provincial decision-making authority. This is necessary but, as has been emphasized throughout this book, not sufficient. Vatican II, in its teachings on the people of God and the sense of the faithful, has planted a seed that will only come to fruition when laypeople, especially women, become active participants in discernment and decision-making authority across the church: in parishes and in diocesan councils, in diocesan, national, and international synods, in the appointments of bishops, and on review boards that hold Catholic leaders, priests, bishops, and religious provincials fully accountable for safeguarding the well-being and honoring the agency of all children, minors, and adults in the communities that comprise today's church. We cannot reasonably hope to move beyond a church of conflict and controversy, but we can find in God a way to confront the church that enables an honest hope and healing.

Notes

Preface

1. For details on accused priests see BishopAccountability, http://www.bishop-accountability.org; on Gilbert Gauthe, see Jason Berry, "The Tragedy of Gilbert Gauthe," *The Times of Acadiana*, part 1, May 23, 1985, part 2, May 30, 1985; a condensed version appeared in the June 7, 1985, edition of *National Catholic Reporter*.

Chapter 1: Begin with the Laments of the Wounded

1. Words of a European abuse survivor, "Words Can Never Be Prescribed," *L'Osservatore Romano*, March 1, 2019, no. 9, 6–7, at 6.

2. County Investigation Grand Jury XXIII, "Report of the Grand Jury," Philadelphia City, PA, Ct. Common Pleas, January 21, 2011, 2–3. Subsequent references will be cited in text.

3. David Finkelhor, *Child Sexual Abuse: New Theory and Research* (New York: Free Press, 1984).

4. The interview of John Delaney was chronicled in the article by Sam Ruland, "When Boy Told of Sexual Abuse, His Parents Asked the Priest Who Raped Him to Counsel Him," *York Daily Record*, September 4, 2018.

5. Office of the Attorney General, "Pennsylvania Grand Jury Report," July 27, 2018, 22, 326.

6. County Investigation Grand Jury, "Report of the Grand Jury," Philadelphia City, PA, Ct. Common Pleas, September 15, 2005, 180.

7. Mary Gail Frawley-O'Dea, *Perversion of Power: Sexual Abuse in the Catholic Church* (Nashville: Vanderbilt University Press, 2007), 6. See John Jay College Report, *The Nature and Scope of Sexual Abuse of Minors by Catholic Priests and Deacons in the United States 1950–2002* (Washington, DC: United States Catholic Conference of Bishops, 2004), 84–93. The John Jay Report will be subsequently cited in the text.

8. John Jay Report, *The Nature and Scope of Sexual Abuse of Minors by Catholic Priests and Deacons in the United States 1950–2002*, 2006 Supplemental Report (Washington, DC: United States Catholic Conference of Bishops, 2006), 8. This report will be subsequently cited in the text.

9. Frawley-O'Dea, *Perversions of Power*, 6.

10. More girls became victims and there was a commensurate decrease of boys beginning in the 1990s through 2002; by 2002 the percentage of male victims was 55.56 and of female victims was 44.44. Whether this trend continued merits further investigation. See Karen J. Terry and Joshua D. Freilich, "Understanding Child Sexual Abuse by Catholic Priests from a Situational Perspective," *Journal of Child Sexual Abuse* 21 (2012): 437–55, at 447, figure 2 on 448.

11. John Jay Report, *Nature and Scope*, 2004, 6, and for complete listing see 55.

12. John Jay Report, *Nature and Scope*, 2004, 55, 73.

13. Grand Jury Reports: Westchester County, NY 6/19/2002; Rockville Centre, NY 2/10/2003; Manchester, NH 3/3/2003; Boston (Reilly Report) 7/23/2003; Portland, ME 2/24/2004; Philadelphia 9/15/2005; Altoona-Johnstown, PA 3/1/2016; Pennsylvania 8/14/2018; grand juries impaneled between 2002 and 2018 but issued no final reports: Phoenix, Cincinnati, Cleveland, and Los Angeles, for example. For more information on grand juries, see chap. 4.

14. Center for Applied Research in the Apostolate (CARA) at Georgetown University, "Nineteen Sixty-Four," ed. Mark M. Grey, August 28, 2018, https://nineteensixty-four.blogspot.com/2018/08/. *ProPublica* released a tally of the credibly accused priests on January 28, 2020, based on the names of priests submitted by dioceses and archdiocese in the United States. This tally is not complete, and it

does not appear to include Eastern Rite Eparchies, nor priests from religious orders. https://projects.propublica.org/credibly-accused. BishopAccountability.org has maintained a "List of Accused Priests Released by Dioceses and Religious Institutes," http://www.bishop-accountability.org/AtAGlance/diocesan_and_order_lists.htm.

15. Mary Gale Frawley-O'Dea, "The John Jay Study: What It Is and What It isn't," *National Catholic Reporter*, July 19, 2011, https://www.ncronline.org/news/accountability/john-jay-study-what-it-and-what-it-isnt. Kathryn Lofton, "Revisited: Sex Abuse and the Study of Religion," *The Immanent Frame*, August 24, 2018, https://tif.ssrc.org/2018/08/24/sex-abuse-and-the-study-of-religion/. Thomas Reese, "The John Jay Report: Facts, Myths and Questions," *America* (March 22, 2004) at https://www.bishop-accountability.org/usccb/natureandscope/general/2004-03-22-Reese-FactsMyths.htm; Thomas Doyle, "'Arrogant Clericalism' Never Assessed by John Jay Report," *Voice in the Desert*, May 21, 2011.

16. Michael Rezendez, "In Mississippi Delta, Catholic Abuse Cases Settle on the Cheap," *Associated Press*, August 27, 2019; PBS, FRONTLINE, "The Silence," producer Tom Curran and reporter Mark Trahant, abuse in Native villages in Alaska (2011), accessed September 3, 2019, https://www.pbs.org/wgbh/pages/frontline/the-silence; Emily Schwing, "After Years of Sexual Abuse in Native Communities, Jesuits Sent Many to Retire on Gonzaga's Campus," PBS/NPR, December 17, 2018, accessed September 3, 2019, https://www.nwpb.org/2018/12/17/after-years-of-sexual-abuse-in-native-communities-jesuits-sent-many-to-retire-on-gonzagas-campus.

17. Kathleen Holscher, "Colonialism and the Crisis Inside the Crisis of Catholic Sexual Abuse," Religion Dispatches, *Rewire News*, August 27, 2018, accessed September 3, 2019, https://rewire.news/religion-dispatches/2018/08/27/from-pa-to-new-mexico-colonialism-and-the-crisis-inside-the-crisis-of-catholic-sexual-abuse. Jack Downey, "Colonialism Is Abuse: Reconsidering Triumphalist Narratives in Catholic Studies," *American Catholic Studies* 130 (2019): 16–20.

18. Robert A. Orsi, "The Study of Religion on the Other Side of Disgust: Modern Catholic Sexuality Is a Dark and Troubled Landscape," *Harvard Divinity Bulletin* 47, nos. 1 and 2 (Spring–Summer 2019): 1–11.

19. Bessel van der Kolk, *The Body Keeps the Score: Brain, Mind, and Body in the Healing of Trauma* (New York: Penguin, 2014), 66.

20. Judith Herman, *Trauma and Recovery: The Aftermath of Violence—from Domestic Abuse to Political Terror* (New York: Basic Books, 2015), 1–2.

21. Herman, *Trauma and Recovery*, 255.

22. Herman, *Trauma and Recovery*, 265, also see 255.

23. Jürgen Moltmann, *The Crucified God: The Cross of Christ as the Foundation and Criticism of Christian Theology*, trans. R. A. Wilson and John Bowden (New York: Harper and Row, 1974); Johann Baptist Metz, *Faith in History and Society*, trans. J. Matthew Ashley (New York: Crossroad, 2007).

24. Jon Sobrino, *Jesus the Liberator: A Historical-Theological View* (Maryknoll, NY: Orbis Books, 1993), 254–71; Jon Sobrino, *The Principle of Mercy: Taking the Crucified People from the Cross* (Maryknoll, NY: Orbis Books, 1994); Jon Sobrino, "Jesuanic Martyrs in the Third World," in *Witnesses to the Kingdom: The Martyrs of El Salvador and the Crucified Peoples* (Maryknoll, NY: Orbis Books, 2003), 119–33.

25. M. Shawn Copeland, *Enfleshing Freedom: Body, Race, and Being* (Maryknoll, NY: Orbis Books, 2010), 1, citing Jeremiah 8:21–23.

26. Copeland, *Enfleshing Freedom*, 116.

27. Copeland, *Enfleshing Freedom*, 126–27. Her christocentric approach to the wounds of slavery and racism is further developed in *Knowing Christ Crucified: The Witness of African American Religious Experience* (Maryknoll, NY: Orbis Books, 2018). Copeland gives new attention to the role of the Spirit in laments in "Breath and Fire," *Commonweal*, July 8, 2020, https://www.commonwealmagazine.org/breath-fire.

28. Jennifer Erin Beste, *God and the Victim: Traumatic Intrusions on Grace and Freedom* (Oxford: Oxford University Press, 2007); Erin Kidd, "The Violation of God in the Body of the World: A Rahnerian Response to Trauma," *Modern Theology* 35 (2019): 663–82. Both Beste and Kidd highlight the contributions of philosopher Judith Butler on body, precarity, and grief, and on Karl Rahner's theology of grace and freedom.

29. Serene Jones, *Trauma and Grace: Theology in a Ruptured World* (Louisville, KY: Westminster John Knox Press, 2009).

30. Jones, *Trauma and Grace*, 53, citing Herman, *Trauma and Recovery*, 155.

31. Bryan Massingale, *Racial Justice and the Catholic Church* (Maryknoll, NY: Orbis Books, 2010), 104–16.

32. Shelly Rambo, *Spirit and Trauma: A Theology of Remaining* (Louisville, KY: Westminster John Knox Press, 2010).

33. Hans Urs von Balthasar, *Mysterium Paschale: The Mystery of Easter*, trans. Aidan Nichols (Edinburgh: T&T Clark, 1990).

Chapter 2:
The Anatomy of a Pathology

1. The John Jay Report, *Causes and Context of Sexual Abuse of Minors by Catholic Priests in the United States, 1950–2010* (2011), 52, also see 53–54, 48–74. Subsequent citations will be parenthetical in the text.

2. Paul Ricœur identifies a pathology of desire in writings of Immanuel Kant and a pathology of duty in the writings of Sigmund Freud, in *Freud and Philosophy: An Essay in Interpretation*, trans. Denis Savage (New Haven, CT: Yale University Press, 1970), 185–86.

3. *Irish Studies: The Ferns Report* (October 2005), *The Ryan Report* (May 20, 2009), *The Murphy Report* (July 2009), *The Cloyne Report* (December 2010), *Australian Report: Royal Commission into Institutional Responses to Child Sexual Abuse* (2012–17).

4. In addition to the Charter, the document *Essential Norms for Diocesan/Eparchial Policies Dealing with Allegations of Sexual Abuse of Minors by Priests or Deacons* was approved by the U.S. Bishops in November 2002 and subsequently recognized by the Holy See, the Vatican.

5. This additional research was conducted by the Center for Applied Research in the Apostolate (CARA), at Georgetown University.

6. John Seitz, "Priests as Persons: An Emotional History of St. John's Seminary, Boston, in the Era of the Council," in *Catholics in the Vatican II Era: Local Histories of a Global Event*, ed. Kathleen

Sprows Cummings, Timothy Matovina, and Robert A. Orsi (New York: Cambridge University Press, 2018), 28–50.

7. John Jay Report (2011), 69, cites a study directed by Eugene Kennedy, *Loyola Psychology Study* (1970), 1, commented on by him in *Bulletins from the Human Side* (newsletter, Nov. 10, 2010).

8. John Jay Report (2011), 70–71, see n. 271.

9. Mary Gail Frawley-O'Dea and Jody Messler Davies, *Treating the Adult Survivor of Childhood Sexual Abuse: A Psychoanalytic Perspective* (New York: Basic Books, 1994).

10. Frawley-O'Dea and Davis, *Treating the Adult Survivor*, 2.

11. Frawley-O'Dea and Davis, *Treating the Adult Survivor*, 4.

12. Frawley-O'Dea and Davis, *Treating the Adult Survivor*, 25.

13. Mary Gail Frawley-O'Dea, *Perversion of Power: Sexual Abuse in the Catholic Church* (Nashville: Vanderbilt University Press, 2007).

14. Frawley-O'Dea, *Perversion of Power*, 23. Subsequent references cited parenthetically in text.

15. A sacrificial interpretation of the death of Jesus Christ offers a common way most believers understand the nature of salvation, but it is not the only way, and the church has never dogmatically defined this doctrine.

16. Marie Keenan, *Child Sexual Abuse and the Catholic Church: Gender, Power, and Organizational Culture* (New York: Oxford University Press, 2011).

17. *Gaudium et Spes* 25. See Margaret Pfeil, "Doctrinal Implications of Magisterial Use of the Language of Social Sin," *Louvain Studies* 27 (2002): 132–52.

18. Second Conference of Latin American Bishops at Medellín, *The Church in the Present-Day Transformation of Latin America in the Light of the Council*, Justice, nos. 16–23, Peace, 1, nos. 1–7, esp. Peace, no. 16, in *The Gospel of Peace and Justice* (Maryknoll, NY: Orbis Books, 1976), 445–76; Third Conference at Puebla in *Puebla and Beyond*, ed. John Eagleson and Philip Scharper, trans. John Drury (Maryknoll, NY: Orbis Books, 1979), 123–285, 128 (nos. 28–30), 132 (no. 73), 191 (no. 487); and Fifth Conference at Aparecida, https://www.celam.org/aparecida/Ingles.pdf, see nos. 92 and 95.

19. This document was issued the same year the Congregation of the Doctrine of the Faith addressed the topic of social sin

in its critique of liberation theology. See Congregation for the Doctrine of the Faith, "Instruction on Certain Aspects of the Theology of Liberation" (1984), section IV, at nos. 13, 14, 15; also CDF clarification on personal and social character of structures and sin, "Instruction on Christian Freedom and Liberation," (1987), nos. 74–75; also see the comment by the International Theological Commission, "Penance and Reconciliation," *Origins* 13, no. 31 (January 12, 1984): 516.

20. John Paul II, *Reconciliatio et Paenitentia* (December 2, 1984), no. 16.

21. John Paul II, *Sollicitudo Rei Socialis* (December 30, 1987), nos. 36–40, at no. 36.

22. John Paul II continued to use the category of social sin in *Centesimus Annus* (May 1, 1991), no. 38, and *Evangelium Vitae* (March 25, 1995), no. 24.

23. John Paul II, *Ut Unum Sint* (May 25, 1995), no. 34

24. Luigi Accatoli, *When a Pope Asks Forgiveness: The* Mea Culpas *of John Paul II* (Boston: St. Paul, 1998); on March 12, 2000, John Paul II led a Day of Pardon prayer service in the Vatican commemorating the sins of the church. The International Theological Commission issued a statement, "Memory and Reconciliation: The Church and the Faults of the Past," December 1999.

25. See the valuable analysis by Brian P. Flanagan, *Stumbling in Holiness: Sin and Sanctity in the Church* (Collegeville, MN: Liturgical Press, 2018).

26. Gregory Baum, "Structures of Sin," in *The Logic of Solidarity: Commentaries on Pope John Paul II's Encyclical on Social Concern*, ed. Gregory Baum and Robert Ellsberg (Maryknoll, NY: Orbis Books, 1989), 110–26, at 113.

27. Pfeil, "Doctrinal Implications of Magisterial Use of the Language of Social Sin," 143.

28. Pfeil, "Magisterial Use of the Language of Social Sin," 152.

29. Keenan, *Child Sexual Abuse and the Catholic Church*, 217–18.

30. Benedict used the term *structures of sin* only once, when he quoted John Paul II's "Message for the Sixteenth World Day of the Sick" (January 11, 2008)." See http://www.vatican.va/content/benedict-xvi/en/messages/sick/documents/hf_ben-xvi_mes _20080111_world-day-of-the-sick-2008.html.

31. See *Caritas in Veritate* 34, 36, 42, and 68, http://w2.vatican
.va/content/benedict-xvi/en/encyclicals/documents/hf_ben-xvi
_enc_20090629_caritas-in-veritate.html. On Benedict's views,
see Daniel J. Daly, "Structures of Virtue and Sin," *New Blackfriars*
2 (2011): 341–57, at 350–52, and Daniel F. Finn, "What Is a Sinful
Social Structure?," *Theological Studies* 77 (2016): 136–64, 139–42,
155.

32. Keenan, *Child Sexual Abuse and the Catholic Church*,
224–28. Emeritus Pope Benedict intervened in the public debate
about the causes of clergy sex abuse on April 11, 2019, by publishing
some reflections that merit consideration in light of the diagno-
ses treated in this chapter: https://www.catholicnewsagency.com/
news/full-text-of-benedict-xvi-the-church-and-the-scandal-of
-sexual-abuse-59639, accessed April 21, 2019.

33. The essay "Corruption and Sin" was originally written in
1991, when he was in "exile" in Córdoba, Argentina, during which
time he reflected on his exercise of leadership, particularly during the time of the "Dirty War" in Argentina (circa 1974–83). Jorge
Mario Bergoglio/Pope Francis, *The Way of Humility* (San Francisco: Ignatius Press, 2013), 7–56.

34. Jorge Mario Bergoglio/Pope Francis, *In Him Alone Is Our
Hope: Spiritual Exercises Given to His Brother Bishops in the Manner of Saint Ignatius of Loyola* (New York: Magnificat, 2013), 134. In
a speech he delivered to the Jesuits gathered for the 36th General
Congregation in November 2016, Francis says, "It is distinctive of
the Society to do things by 'thinking with the Church.'...To do this
peacefully and joyfully, given *the sins we perceive within ourselves
and in the structures we have created*, entails carrying the cross and
experiencing poverty and humiliation, the locus in which Ignatius encourages us to choose between patiently enduring them
and desiring them." "Address to the 36th General Congregation,"
https://jesuits.eu/images/docs/GC_36_Documents.pdf, 42–43.

35. *Evangelii Gaudium* 53.

36. Roger Landry quotes Cardinal Bergoglio's 2011 Interview
with an Argentinian Catholic news agency in "Pope Francis and
the Reform of the Laity," *National Catholic Register*, posted April
12, 2013, accessed March 13, 2021, https://catholicpreaching.com/
wp/pope-francis-and-the-reform-of-the-laity-national-catholic
-register-april-12-2013/.

37. Bergoglio, "Pope Francis and the Reform of the Laity." Francis's view on the clericalization of the laity is different from John Paul II in *Christifideles Laici* 23.

38. *Evangelii Gaudium* 93–97, 102.

39. Pope Francis's addresses on the examinations of conscience and the reform of the curia took place in December 2014, 2015, 2016, 2017, 2018 (in which he spoke of sin of sexual abuse and the abuse of power and corruption), and 2019 on the structural reform of the curia.

40. Pope Francis, "The Roman Curia and the Body of Christ" (2014).

41. Francis, "The Roman Curia and the Body of Christ."

42. Pope John Paul II, *On Social Concern* (December 30, 1987), no. 37.

Chapter 3: Prophetic Voices, Protests, and Movements

1. Pope Francis, *Evangelii Gaudium* 259; Pope Francis, "Greeting to the Synod Fathers during the First General Congregation of the Third Extraordinary General Assembly of the Synod of Bishops," October 6, 2014; Pope Francis, *Apostolic Exhortation, Gaudete et Exsultate* (2018), 129–39.

2. Michel Foucault, "Discourse and Truth: The Problematization of Parrhesia," lecture, University of California at Berkeley, October–November 1983, http://foucault.info/documents/parrhesia/.

3. Brian J. Clites, "Breaking the Silence: The Catholic Sexual Abuse Movement in Chicago" (PhD diss., Northwestern University, 2015), 14.

4. Jason Berry, "The Tragedy of Gilbert Gauthe" (two parts), *The Times of Acadiana*, 23 and 30, May 1985; a condensed version, *National Catholic Reporter*, June 7, 1985.

5. On Patricia Crowley and her husband, Patrick, see Clites, "Breaking the Silence," 129–41.

6. For the history of SNAP, see "SNAP Mission Statement," SNAP, accessed April 20, 2019, http://www.snapnetwork.org/about.

7. Clites, "Breaking the Silence," 266.

8. Reuters, "Catholics Hoping to Shift Bit of Power from Pulpit to Pew," *New York Times*, July 21, 2002, 21.

9. D'Antonio and Pogorelc interviewed founders and leaders of VOTF in 2003–4 and sent surveys in 2004–5 to members, which informed their publication, *Voices of the Faithful: Loyal Catholics Striving for Change* (New York: Herder and Herder, 2007).

10. For Catholic critics of investigative reporting, see David De Cosse, "Freedom of the Press and Catholic Social Thought: Reflections on the Sexual Abuse Scandal in the Catholic Church in the United States," *Theological Studies* 68 (2007): 865–89.

11. These examples draw from the reports compiled by BishopAccountability, the U.S.-based internet platform for making available information about cases of clerical sexual abuse of minors that was started in 2003. See http://www.bishop-accountability.org.

12. "Abuse in the Catholic Church: Boston Globe Team Discusses Working with Victims," Dart Center for Journalism and Trauma, April 8, 2003, accessed May 2, 2019, https://dartcenter.org/content/abuse-in-catholic-church.

13. Pope Francis responds to Nicole Winfield's question about the sexual abuse of consecrated women in the church at the end of the "Transcript of Pope Francis's In-Flight Press Conference," *Catholic News Agency*, February 5, 2019, https://www.catholicnewsagency.com/news/full-text-of-pope-francis-in-flight-press-conference-from-abu-dhabi-50036.

14. See Patrick Hornbeck, "*Respondeat Superior* Vicarious Liability for Clergy Sexual Abuse: Four Approaches," *Buffalo Law Review* 68, no. 4 (2020): 975–1036. Hornbeck has generously responded to my questions about legal issues; any errors are my own.

15. "Data on the Crisis: The Human Toll" and "List of Accused Priests by Dioceses and Religious Institutes," BishopAccountability, http://www.bishopaccountability.org. For cross-tracking, see *ProPublica*, https://projects.propublica.org/credibly-accused, and background article, Mark Smith, "Catholic Leaders Promised Transparency about Child Abuse. They Haven't Delivered. Sins of Omission," January 28, 2020, https://www.propublica.org/article/

catholic-leaders-promised-transparency-about-child-abuse-they
-havent-delivered.

16. State attorneys general are elected in forty-three states, appointed by the governor in five states, or by the state Supreme Court in Tennessee, or by the state legislature in Maine; the District of Columbia, Guam, and Northern Mariana Islands elect the attorneys general, whereas the attorneys general in American Samoa, Puerto Rico, and the U.S. Virgin Islands are appointed by the governor.

17. Grand jury reports: Westchester County, NY, June 19, 2002; Rockville Centre, NY, February 10, 2003; Manchester, NH, March 3, 2003; Boston (Reilly Report), July 23, 2003; Portland, ME, February 24, 2004; Philadelphia, September 15, 2005; Altoona-Johnstown, PA, March 1, 2016; Pennsylvania, August 14, 2018.

18. Phoenix, Cincinnati, Cleveland, and Los Angeles, for example.

19. Peter Steinfels has stated that there are more than a dozen in "Vehemently Misleading: The PA Grand-Jury Report: Not What It Seems," *Commonweal* 146, no. 2 (January 25, 2019): 13–26, at 26.

20. Timothy D. Lytton treats clergy sexual abuse as an institutional failure needing policy reform in *Holding Bishops Accountable* (Cambridge, MA: Harvard University Press, 2008), 81–160.

21. The 2005 Philadelphia Grand Jury Report did indict specific priests pertaining to specific criminal behavior.

22. Lytton treats these three recommendations, as does Steinfels, who also identified a fourth recommendation of "a civil window" of two years "during which victims can sue dioceses for abuse not just if accusers are under thirty," thereby financially damaging not the perpetrators of these offenses but Catholic parishes, charities, and dioceses, which is proposed in the Pennsylvania report as included in California, Minnesota, Hawaii, and Delaware (Steinfels, "Vehemently Missing," 25).

23. See Lytton, *Holding Bishops Accountable*, 84–94.

24. Cathleen Kaveny, *Prophecy without Contempt: Religious Discourse in the Public Square* (Cambridge, MA: Harvard University Press, 2016), 126–80, 239–81; on grand juries, see 322–27; on irony in Jonah and in public discourse, 397–418. Also see Kaveny, "A Matter of Justice, Not Merely Chastity," *The Immanent Frame*,

https://tif.ssrc.org/2019/02/19/a-matter-of-justice-not-merely
-chastity/.

25. Peter Steinfels's argument about the deficiency of grand jury protocols for providing an opportunity for bishops to defend their actions was advanced before the Pennsylvania Supreme Court by numerous bishops. See, e.g., the opinions of July 27, 2018, and December 3, 2018, http://www.pacourts.us/news-and-statistics/cases-of-public-interest/fortieth-statewide-investigating-grand-jury, accessed May 19, 2019.

Chapter 4:
The Responses of Bishops

1. Peter Steinfels, PA Grand-Jury Report: Not What It Seems," *Commonweal* 146, no. 2 (January 25, 2019): 13–26.

2. A group was established in 2003 to hold bishops accountable through the use of a website, BishopAccountability: BishopAccountability.org. This website provides links to primary materials, court records, grand jury reports, and documents accused and convicted clerical sexual abusers and bishops.

3. Barbara Susan Balboni, "Through the 'Lens' of the Organizational Culture Perspective: A Descriptive Study of American Bishops' Understanding of Clergy Sexual Molestation of Children Adolescents" (PhD diss., Northeastern University, 1998), 161–66, 277–79.

4. See Bradford E. Hinze, *Practices of Dialogue in the Church: Aims and Obstacles, Lessons and Laments* (New York: Crossroad, 2006).

5. John Jay Report, *The Causes and Context of Sexual Abuse of Minors by Catholic Priests in the United States, 1950–2010* (2011), 80–91.

6. The percentage of priests suspended based on whether the allegations were credible (241 priests/45.9%), noncredible (17 priests/8.9%), substantiated (852 priests/45.5%), and unsubstantiated (171 priests/20.8%) as reported on surveys submitted by

dioceses and religious communities; for statistics and trends, see John Jay Report, *Causes and Context* (2004), 95–98.

7. See Balboni, "Through the 'Lens' of the Organizational Cultural Perspective," 208–14. The National Review Board offered comparable advice about lawyers eight years after Benardin died in "A Report on the Crisis in the Catholic Church in the United States," USCCB, Washington, DC, 2004, 119–23.

8. Everett M. Rogers, *The Diffusion of Innovations*, 5th ed. (New York: Free Press, 2003).

9. John Jay Report, *Causes and Context*, 84–85.

10. F. Ray Mouton, JD, Rev. Thomas P. Doyle, OP, JCD, and Rev. Michael R. Peterson, "The Problem of Sexual Molestation by Roman Catholic Clergy: Meeting the Problem in a Comprehensive and Responsible Manner," (cited as the Manual), December 27, 1985; "Notes on the Manual," and Thomas Doyle, "A Short History of 'The Manual,'" available at https://www.bishop-accountability .org/reports/1985_06_09_Doyle_Manual/.

11. See John Jay Report (2011), 77; 137n281.

12. National Catholic Conference of Bishops, "Statements of the NCCB and the USCC on the Subject of the Sexual Abuse of Children by Priests 1988–1992" (unpublished report, November 19, 1992), 10–11, quoted in John Jay Report (2011), 82.

13. For further information on the model and its application, see John Jay Report (2011), 85–86.

14. John Jay Report (2011), 84.

15. John Jay Report (2011), 86–87.

16. Here I offer an abridged statement of nine of the seventeen promises.

17. There have been revisions of the Charter in 2006, 2011, and 2018, and Norms have been revised in 2006; for criticisms and proposals, see Dan Morris-Young, "Only Minor Changes Proposed for Abuse Charter Revisions," *National Catholic Reporter*, June 15, 2011.

18. Ladislas Orsy, "Bishops' Norms: Commentary and Evaluation," *Boston College Law Review* 44, no. 4 (2003): 1023.

19. Avery Cardinal Dulles, "Rights of Accused Priests: Toward a Revision of the Dallas Charter and the Essential Norms," *America*, June 21, 2004.

20. John Paul II, apostolic exhortation, *Christifideles Laici: On the Vocation and the Mission of the Lay Faithful in the Church and in the World* (December 30, 1988).

21. *Instruction on Certain Questions Regarding the Collaboration of the Non-ordained Faithful in the Sacred Ministry of Priests*, issued by eight Vatican offices (Boston: Pauline Books & Media, 1998).

22. John Paul II, apostolic exhortation, *Pastores Dabo Vobis* (March 15, 1992).

23. John Paul II, *motu proprio, Sacramentorum Sanctitatis Tuetela*, 2001.

24. Congregation for Catholic Education, "Instruction Concerning the Criteria for the Discernment of Vocations with Regard to Persons with Homosexual Tendencies in View of Their Admission to the Seminary and to Holy Orders," November 2005.

25. John Paul II spoke about the challenges of the abuse in the midst of only revelations published by the *Boston Globe* in "Address of John Paul II to the Cardinals of the United States, April 23, 2002," http://www.vatican.va/content/john-paul-ii/en/speeches/2002/april/documents/hf_jp-ii_spe_20020423_usa-cardinals.html.

26. Pope Benedict XVI, "Pastoral Letter to the Catholics of Ireland," March 19, 2010, no. 11, http://www.vatican.va/content/benedict-xvi/en/letters/2010/documents/hf_ben-xvi_let_20100319_church-ireland.html.

27. Benedict XVI, "Pastoral Letter to the Catholics of Ireland," no. 4.

28. Pope Benedict XVI, Address to U.S. Bishops, April 16, 2008.

29. Congregation for the Doctrine of the Faith, "Letter to the Bishops of the Catholic Church on the Pastoral Care of Homosexual Persons," signed by Prefect Cardinal Joseph Ratzinger, October 1, 1986, see nos. 10–14. Congregation for the Doctrine of the Faith, "Considerations Regarding Proposals to Give Legal Recognition to Unions between Homosexual Persons," signed by Prefect Cardinal Joseph Ratzinger, March 28, 2003, no. 11.

30. Lieven Boeve, "Why Benedict XVI Resigned: Cognitive Dissonance," in *Theology at the Crossroads of University, Church and Society: Dialogue, Difference and Catholic Identity* (London: Bloomsbury, 2016), 221–34.

31. On April 10, 2019, Emeritus Pope Benedict, after the meeting of the presidents of episcopal conferences convened in Rome in February 2019, published a letter offering his commentary on the state of the discussion on clergy sex abuse crises, reiterating his long-held convictions on the role of the personal sin of clergy and secularization.

32. On Jorge Bergoglio/Pope Francis, see J. Matthew Ashley, *Renewing Theology: Ignatian Spirituality and Karl Rahner, Ignacio Ellacuría, and Pope Francis* (South Bend, IN: University of Notre Dame Press, 2022).

33. Priyanka Boghani, "Pope Francis Holds First Meeting with Abuse Victims, Public Broadcasting Service," July 7, 2014.

34. Joshua J. McElwee, "For Only Second Time, Francis Meets Abuse Survivors, Says 'God Weeps,'" *National Catholic Reporter*, September 27, 2015.

35. Joshua J. McElwee, drawing on information provided by *La Civiltà Cattolica*, reported that "Pope Francis Says He Meets Almost Weekly with Abuse Victims," *National Catholic Reporter*, February 15, 2018. See also Joshua J. McElwee, "Francis Meets Eight Irish Survivors, Reportedly Calls Abuse Cover-Up 'Caca,'" *National Catholic Reporter*, August 25, 2018.

36. Joshua J. McElwee, "Pope to Meet with Second Group of Abuse Survivors from Chile," *National Catholic Reporter*, May 23, 2018.

37. Pope Francis, "To the Pilgrim People of God in Chile," *Catholic News Agency*, accessed June 20, 2019, http://catholicnewsagency.com/news/full-text-of-pope-francis-letter-to-the-church-in-chile-35580.

38. Laurie Goodstein and Sharon Otterman, "He Preyed on Men Who Wanted to Be Priests. Then He Became a Cardinal," *New York Times*, July 16, 2018.

39. Joshua J. McElwee, "Francis Says He May Reconsider Convicted Cardinal's Resignation after Appeal," *National Catholic Reporter*, March 31, 2019. He summarizes his views on the November 2018 Proposal on Metropolitans, citing January 1, 2019, letter to U.S. Bishops.

40. "Americans See Catholic Clergy Sex Abuse as an Ongoing Problem," Pew Research Center, June 11, 2019, https://www

.pewforum.org/2019/06/11/americans-see-catholic-clergy-sex
-abuse-as-an-ongoing-problem/.

41. Pope Francis, Closing Address, "The Protection of Minors in the Church," February 24, 2019.

42. Rachel Donadio, "Survivors of Church Abuse Want Zero Tolerance. The Pope Offers Context," *The Atlantic*, February 24, 2019; Austen Ivereigh, "Vatican Summon Sex Abuse," *Commonweal*, March 22, 2019.

43. *Code of Canon Law*, canons 435–36; see Vatican II's *Christus Dominus* 39–40.

44. Pope Francis, motu proprio *Vos Estis Lux Mundi*, May 7, 2019. Article 1, §1.b.

45. Pope Francis motu proprio "On the Protection of Minors and Vulnerable Persons," which applies to the Vatican, issued on June 1, 2019.

Chapter 5:
Changes Long Resisted

1. Reese Dunklin, Mitch Weiss, and Matt Sedensky, "AP: Catholic Boards Hailed as Fix for Sex Abuse Often Fail," November 20, 2019, https://apnews.com/66ffb032675b4e599eb77c0875718dd4.

2. These are representative works by the three most prominent U.S. authors on this subject: Richard Sipe, *Sex, Priests, and Power: Anatomy of a Crisis* (New York: Brunner/Mazel, Inc., 1995); Eugene Kennedy with V. J. Heckler, *The Loyola Psychological Study of the Ministry and Life of the American Priest* (Washington, DC: National Conference of Catholics Bishops, 1971); Donald B. Cozzens, *The Changing Face of the Priesthood* (Collegeville, MN: The Liturgical Press, 2000).

3. Robert L. Anello, "Priestly Celibacy and Identity: The Rocky Reception of Vatican II's *Presyterorum Ordinis*," *U.S. Catholic Historian* 32 (2014): 27–53.

4. Anello, "Priestly Celibacy," 33. Since Eastern Rite Catholic bishops were participating in the council and to avoid pitting married and celibate clergy, the document praised celibate priests,

without denying the "highest merits" of married clergy (among Eastern Catholics).

5. Pope Paul VI, *Sacerdotalis Caelibatus* (1967), and the Synod of Bishops, *The Synod of Bishops: The Ministerial Priesthood; Justice in the World*, 2nd ed. (Washington, DC: National Conference of Catholic Bishops, 1972).

6. Pope John Paul II, *Pastores Dabo Vobis*, 1992.

7. Pope John Paul II, *Pastores Dabo Vobis* 29.

8. *On Heaven and Earth: Pope Francis on Faith, Family, and the Church in the Twenty-First Century*, trans. Alejandro Bermudez and Howard Goodman (New York: Image Books, 2013).

9. Cited by David Gibson, "Book Reveals New Pope's Views on Celibacy, Abuse Crisis," *USA Today*, March 20, 2013. The book mentioned is *On Heaven and Earth*.

10. This occurred in 2014 in a conversation Francis had with Bishop Edward Kräutler, bishop of Xingu in the Brazilian rain forest (Christa Pongratz-Lippitt, "Pope Asks Rainforest Bishop to Help on Encyclical," *The Tablet*, April 10, 2014) and again in 2017.

11. Prop. 111: "Considering that legitimate diversity does not harm the communion and unity of the Church, but manifests and serves it (LG 13; OE 6) which gives witness of the plurality of existing rites and disciplines, we propose to establish criteria and dispositions on the part of the competent authority, in the framework of *Lumen Gentium* 26, to ordain as priests suitable men recognized by the community, that have a fruitful Permanent Diaconate and receive appropriate formation for the presbyterate, being able to have a legitimately constituted and stable family, to sustain the life of the Christian community through preaching the Word and the celebration of the Sacraments in the most remote areas of the Amazonian region. In this connection, some were in favor of a universal treatment of this subject." Approved by a vote of 128 to 41. "Amazon Synod: Zenit Translation of Final Document, Introduction and Chapter One," Zenit, October 30, 2019, accessed January 7, 2020, https://zenit.org/articles/amazon-synod-zenit-translation-of-final-document-introduction-and-chapter-one.

12. Pope Francis, *Querida Amazonia*, February 2, 2020, nos. 85–90.

13. This text from Pope Francis was included in an article by Antonio Spadaro, "Francis's Government: What Is the Driving

Force of His Pontificate?" *La Civiltà Cattolica*, September 21, 2020, https://www.laciviltacattolica.com/francis-government-what-is -the-driving-force-of-his-pontificate/, see 4–5.

14. Mary Anne Case, "The Role of the Popes in the Invention of Complementarity and the Vatican's Anathematization of Gender," *Religion and Gender* 6 (2016): 155–72.

15. Eight dicasteries of the curia issued "On Certain Questions Regarding the Collaboration of the Non-ordained Faithful in the Sacred Ministry of Priest," 1997.

16. Before Vatican II, men preparing for priesthood were ordained to the office of diaconate (*deacon* in Greek means "one who serves"), for a year or more before being ordained a priest. At Vatican II, the bishops retrieved the permanent diaconate state for celibate men, or for men thirty-five years or older who are married. Deacons are able to baptize, bless marriages, lead funeral services, and can read from the Scriptures and preach in the context of mass.

17. Chris Hedges, "Documents Allege Abuse of Nuns by Priests," *New York Times*, March 21, 2001, Section A, p. 10. Jason Horowitz and Elizabeth Dias, "Pope Acknowledges Nuns Were Sexually Abused by Priests and Bishops," *New York Times*, February 5, 2019, https://www.nytimes.com/2019/02/05/world/europe/pope-nuns-sexual-abuse.html.

18. Joshua J. McElwee, "Francis: Women Deacons Commission Gave Split Report on Their Role in Early Church," *National Catholic Reporter*, May 7, 2019.

19. Proposition 103 was approved by a vote of 137 to 33.

20. *Querida Amazonia* 100.

21. A new commission to study women deacons was announced on June 28, 2020. Sr. Bernadette Mary Reis, "Pope Institutes New Commission to Study Women Deacons," *Vatican News*, April 2020.

22. For more details, see Myriam Wijlems, "Women in the Church: A Canonical Perspective," *L'Osservatore Romano*, January 2, 2017.

23. Joshua J. McElwee, "Francis Appoints First Woman to Managerial Role at Vatican's Secretariat of State," *National Public Radio*, January 15, 2020.

24. Homosexuality was one of many issues addressed by The Congregation for the Doctrine of the Faith in their *Declaration on Certain Questions Concerning Sexual Ethics*, no. 8, 1975.

25. The Congregation of the Doctrine of the Faith in "Letter to the Bishops of the Catholic Church on the Pastoral Care of Homosexual Persons," no. 3. The documents distinction between homosexual acts and inclinations or tendencies led to many positive interpretations of the latter. As a result, this new document clarified that the distinction between a homosexual condition or tendency and individual actions are both "'intrinsically disordered,' and able in no case to be approved of" (1986, no. 3).

26. Thomas G. Plante, "No, Homosexuality Is Not a Risk Factor for the Sexual Abuse of Children," *America*, October 22, 2018, https://www.americamagazine.org/faith/2018/10/22/no-homo sexuality-not-risk-factor-sexual-abuse-children. Thomas G. Plante, "Clergy Sexual Abuse in the Roman Catholic Church: Dispelling Eleven Myths and Separating Facts from Fiction," *Spirituality in Clinical Practice*, http://dx.doi.org/10.1037/scp0000209.

27. John Jay Report, *Causes and Context of Sexual Abuse of Minors by Catholic Priests in the United States, 1950–2010* (Washington, DC: United States Catholic Conference of Bishops, 2011), 52–74, at 62–64, 74. Also see David Gibson, "New Catholic Sex Abuse Findings: Gay Priests Are Not the Problem," *Politics Daily*, November 18, 2009, https://www.bishop-accountability.org/news2009/11_12/2009_11_18_PoliticsDaily_NewCatholic.htm.

Chapter 6:
Can We Find a Way Together?

1. See the International Theological Commission, "Synodality in the Life and Mission of the Church," March 2, 2018, http://www.vatican.va/roman_curia/congregations/cfaith/cti_documents/rc_cti_20180302_sinodalita_en.html.

2. Bishop Brendan Leahy, "Together in Mission: A Time to Begin Again," Pastoral Letter Convoking a Diocesan Synod (August

2014), Limerick Diocesan Synod Website, http://www.synod2016 .com.

3. Bishop Brendan Leahy, "Moving Forward Together in Hope" (December 8, 2016), Limerick Diocesan Pastoral Plan 2016–2026, the 2016 Diocesan Synod, http://www.synod2016.com.

4. Bishop Brendan Leahy's announcement of the synod, September 28, 2014, http://www.synod2016.com/our-journey/ a-synod-for-limerick-diocese/full-text-of-a-letter-from-bishop -brendan-announcing-the-synodal-process.

5. Bishop Leahy, "Moving Forward Together in Hope." A Progress Report was issued in 2017: http://www.synod2016.com/ sy/assets/File/2017/Limerick%20Diocese%20Pastoral%20Plan %202016-2026%20Progress%20Report%20-%20September %202017_vf.pdf.

6. The summary of the first phase of the Australian Plenary Council can be found at https://plenarycouncil.catholic.org.au/ wp-content/uploads/2019/09/FINAL-BOOK-v7-online-version -LISTEN-TO-WHAT-THE-SPIRIT-IS-SAYING.pdf.

7. See the Special Report commissioned by the Australian Bishops Conference, *Light of the Southern Cross: Promoting Co-responsible Governance in the Catholic Church in Australia*, May 1, 2020, https://www.associationofcatholicpriests.ie/wp-content/ uploads/2020/06/03-FINAL-Southern-Cross-Report-010520 -SinglePage_1.pdf. The document's assets and limitations are well stated by Richard R. Gaillardetz, "A Promising Roadmap for Ecclesial Reform and Conversion," *La Croix International*, June 4, 2020, https://international.la-croix.com/news/religion/a-promising -roadmap-for-ecclesial-reform-and-conversion/12499.

8. Australia Plenary Council, *Instrumentum Laboris: Continuing the Journey* (February 25, 2021), https://plenarycouncil .catholic.org.au/wp-content/uploads/2021/02/IL-document -single-pages.pdf.

9. For a brief history of the Zentralkommittee der deutschen Katholik, see "Die Geschichte des ZdK," https://www.zdk.de/ueber -uns/blick-in-die-geschichte.

10. For the composition of the synodal assembly, see the Statutes of the Synodal Way, https://dbk.de/fileadmin/Synodalerweg/ Dokumente_Reden_Beitraege/Satzung-des-Synodalen-Weges .pdf.

11. "Schreiben von Papst Franziskus an das Pilgernde Volk Gottes in Deutschland," no. 3, http://w2.vatican.va/content/ francesco/de/letters/2019/documents/papa-francesco_20190629 _lettera-fedeligermania.html.

12. "Schreiben von Papst Franziskus an das Pilgernde Volk Gottes in Deutschland," no. 5, "Dass nämlich eine der ersten und größten Versuchungen im kirchlichen Bereich darin bestehe zu glauben, dass die Lösungen der derzeitigen und zukünftigen Probleme ausschließlich auf dem Wege der Reform von Strukturen, Organisationen und Verwaltung zu erreichen sei, dass diese aber schlussendlich in keiner Weise die vitalen Punkte berühren, die eigentlich der Aufmerksamkeit bedürfen."

13. For background, see Christa Pongratz-Lippitt, "From the Letter of Pope Francis to the Germans: The Origins, Reception and Various Interpretations of the Pope's Views on the German Synod," *La Croix International*, September 30, 2019.

14. "Satzung des Synodalen Weges," Article 11, No. 2, Der Synodale Weg, accessed November 30, 2019, https://dbk.de/ fileadmin/Synodalerweg/Dokumente_Reden_Beitraege/Satzung -des-Synodalen-Weges.pdf.

15. "Satzung des Synodalen Weges," Article 11, No. 5, Der Synodale Weg.

16. "ZdK-Vizepräsidentin wirbt für Zustimmung zum Synodalen Weg," ZdK, November 22, 2019, accessed November 30, 2019, https://www.zdk.de/veroeffentlichungen/pressemeldungen/ detail/ZdK-Vizepraesidentin-wirbt-fuer-Zustimmung-zum -Synodalen-Weg-1285a.

17. "ZdK-Vizepräsidentin wirbt für Zustimmung zum Synodalen Weg," ZdK.

18. Estelle Zinsstag and Marie Keenan, "Restorative Responses to Sexual Violence: An Introduction," in *Restorative Responses to Sexual Violence: Legal, Social and Therapeutic Dimensions*, ed. Estelle Zinsstag and Marie Keenan, Routledge Frontiers of Criminal Justice (New York: Routledge, 2017), 27–36, at 31.

19. Stephen J. Pope and Janine P. Geske, "Anger, Forgiveness, and Restorative Justice in Light of Clerical Sexual Abuse and Its Cover-Up," *Theological Studies* 80 (2019): 611–31.

20. Theo Gavrielides, "Clergy Sexual Abuse and the Restorative Justice Dialogue," *Journal of Church and State* 55 (2013): 617–39, at 623.

21. The most valuable analysis of these issues is offered by sociologist Michele Dillon, *Postsecular Catholicism: Relevance and Renewal* (New York: Oxford University Press, 2018); statistical findings are analyzed by the PEW Research Center, "Americans See Catholic Clergy Abuse as an Ongoing Problem," June 11, 2019, https://www.pewforum.org/2019/06/11/americans-see-catholic-clergy-sex-abuse-as-an-ongoing-problem/; Pew Research Center, "In U.S. Decline of Christianity Continues at Rapid Pace," October 17, 2019, https://www.pewforum.org/2019/10/17/in-u-s-decline-of-christianity-continues-at-rapid-pace/.

22. On the diverse types of church teachings, see Richard R. Gaillardetz, *By What Authority? Foundations for Understanding Authority in the Church*, rev. ed. (Collegeville, MN: Liturgical Press, 2018), 154–75, 200–218.

23. On the history of the term and its usage, see William Henn, OFMCap, "The Hierarchy of Truths Twenty Years Later," *Theological Studies* 58 (1987): 439–71.

24. Ormond Rush on Karl Rahner's position on a person's concrete or personal catechism in *The Eyes of Faith: The Sense of the Faith and the Church's Reception of Revelation* (Washington, DC: Catholic University of America Press, 2009), 222, 228, 238–39, 265–66.

25. Peter De Mey, "Die Hermeneutik des differenzierten/differenzierenden Konsensus: einmaliges Zugeständnis oder breit einsatzbare ökumenische Methode für die römisch-katholische Kirche?," in *Auf dem Weg zur Gemeinschaft: 50 Jahre internationaler evangelisch-lutherisch/römischen-katholischer Dialog*, ed. André Peter Birmelé and Wolfgang Thönissen (Leipzig: Bonifatius Verlag—Evangelische Verlagsanstalt, 2018), 385–403.

26. Pope John XXIII, Encyclical on "Truth, Unity, and Peace, in a Spirit of Charity," June 29, 1959, "In necessariis unitas, in dubiis libertas, in omnibus caritas."

Index

Index